Beautiful Americas

AN NCPA ANTHOLOGY

A collection of fiction and nonfiction
travel/vacation stories
by NCPA authors

Nan Mahon, Elaine Faber, Susan Beth Furst, Bobbie
Fite, Jackie Alcalde Marr, Sharon S Darrow, Lorna
Griess, Tom Kando, Bob Irelan, M.L. Hamilton,
Denise Lee Branco, Danita Moon, Linda Villatore,
Norma Jean Thornton, RoseMary Covington Morgan,
Loren Diaz, Daniel Schmitt, A.K. Buckroth, Patricia E.
Canterbury, Roberta "Berta" Davis, Sandra D.
Simmer, Scott Charles, Ronald Javor, Dave Todd,
Barbara Klide, Cheryl Anne Stapp, Ellen Osborn,
Barbara Young, Christine L. Villa, Charlene Johnson

BEAUTIFUL AMERICAS

A collection of fiction and nonfiction travel and vacation stories by NCPA writers

Published by
Samati Press
P.O. Box 214673
Sacramento, CA 95821
www.sharonsdarrow.com

This book is independently published by Samati Press in arrangement with individual members of Northern California Publishers & Authors: www.norcalpa.org.

Printed in the United States of America

ISBN: (paperback): 978-1-949125-41-2
         (ebook): 978-1-949125-42-9
LCCN: 2022921545

TABLE OF CONTENTS

THE MYSTIQUE OF ROUTE 66

NAN MAHON

t's that summer after high school graduation when a sense of freedom hits. Some guys may think of becoming a Marine, or simply surfing on ocean waves for a season. For me, there were two great 20th century writers who shaped my summer plan. In the fall, I would be a freshman at the University of Kansas, working on a major in English literature. But for the next three months, I would follow the authors, John Steinbeck and Jack Kerouac, long dead now, experiencing history on The Mother Road: Route 66.

I loaded my four-year old Toyota RAV4 with camping gear and books while my mother shoved bags of groceries in the back seat. My father stood by, giving advice.

"Keep your cell phone charged and use your AAA card if you need help. Keep the gas tank full. You got a jack and a good spare?"

My mother fretted. "Ronnie, please don't pick up hitch hikers. I wish you were not going alone."

"Not alone, Ma. I got Gus with me." The German Shepard looked up as I mentioned his name.

With the usual hugs and good-byes, the dog and I hit the open road with great expectations and Maroon 5 playing on the radio.

We left Kansas and headed for Springfield, Missouri, about 520 miles from the historic highway's starting point in Chicago, Illinois. As I visited the Springfield Museum, I began to understand the long, two-lane strip of asphalt carried the destiny, dreams, and despair of many before me. Members of my own family were part of the big migration several generations ago. My dad's father would often tell stories of being a small boy with his family making the journey to California and the hardships they overcame on

1

the way.

I thought of him now as I bought the guide book and road map. Route 66 covered eight states and 2,500 miles. Gus and I were ready. Back in the RAV4, I ate one of Mom's sandwiches and traced the thin line I would travel on the back road of history.

It was evening when I rolled through Tulsa. I kept going until the city lights were distant behind me. The red dirt lay in mounds beside the highway just as it had when the winds blew the Oklahoma top soil across the farmland and kept blowing until the sky was dark with it and everything was covered with dirt. Steinbeck wrote about it, saying *"to the red country of Oklahoma the last rain came gently."*

I pulled down a country road and made camp. More of Mom's sandwiches and a bottle of water under the stars felt pretty good right then. I had brought a copy of Steinbeck's *The Grapes of Wrath*, the Pulitzer Prize winning novel that chronicled the reluctant journey of displaced migrants on this highway. I sat in a camp chair and read by lantern, transported to a distant era where the Joad family piled their few belongings onto an old truck, preparing to leave the only home they knew. Deep into the story, I heard Gus's whine and a baby cry.

A woman appeared out of the shadows, carrying a small child on her hip. She just seemed to materialize there without a sound. Her dress was old and dirty and she was wearing shoes without socks. I felt as if I was in one of those black and white movies from the 40s. Or maybe the 30s, like the Joad family.

"Can you spare some food, sir?" she asked.

Without a word, I handed her the remainder of Mom's sandwiches and cookies. She sat in the dirt and ate, feeding the child scraps.

"Thank you kindly," she said. I could see she was crying. "My man went off to California to find work in the fields there. Since the dust dried up all the ground here, we lost our farm to the bank."

She drank the water I gave her and I handed her a bunch of bananas. She smashed one in her fingers and fed the baby.

"We ain't no slackers," she said. "We are hard workers, but there ain't no work to be had. If you goin' to California, maybe you will meet up with my husband and tell him we need him. Name of William Brady. My name's Mary."

I nodded and asked, "What year is it?"

"Why, it's 1935. God bless you, sir." She faded back into the shadows.

That wasn't real, I told myself. But, in a parallel universe, history lives on in the places where it takes place. Great battles, inspiring speeches, and events that change the world live on in the edges of time.

It was hours before I fell asleep, hugging Gus to me like a child with a stuffed teddy bear. So, this was what John Steinbeck tried to tell Americans in his novel, *The Grapes of Wrath*. He was ridiculed and his book banned as he exposed the human tragedy and abuse of desperate workers during the Great Dust Bowl. Years later, he was awarded both the Nobel and Pulitzer Prizes for his work.

The next day, I was strangely relieved when Gus and I left Oklahoma and dropped into Texas. The road was long and flat, dotted with watermelon stands, water tanks, windmills and Burma Shave signs. I ate in small diners where truckers once stopped. They were diners such as the ones Steinbeck wrote about in his book. The locals were friendly and ready to talk about the old highway and the stories handed down to them by family.

It took two days to get across Texas and into New Mexico with its rocky, rough, dry blistering heat. I remembered the pictures of old cars with water bags hanging from the radiators belching steam, and drivers hoping to make it to the next station before they went dry. We made camp under stars beside green cactus on grainy dirt. Coyotes howled and I kept Gus close for his safety as well as mine.

Starting out the next day, I was thinking of Kerouac and reciting some of his abstract Beatnik poetry from memory. Closer to Gallup, Navajo women dressed in velvet blouses and long cotton skirts spread blankets on boulders to sell

3

silver and turquoise jewelry, and woven rugs. Again, I was conscious of being out of place in time, that feeling of a noir movie of the 40s or 50s. This was Kerouac's time and place; I knew I was no longer in the present.

The next day we made Arizona and the exquisite Painted Desert. As if on cue, I found a jazz station on my car radio just as Jack Kerouac and Dean Moriarty had in his memoir *On the Road*. The sounds of muted trumpets and soft saxophones filled the Toyota. I rolled down the windows so wind could carry the music across the waste land.

It was near the Arizona Stateline that I saw the girl beside the road with her thumb in the air. I pulled over and nudged Gus into the back seat.

She yanked open the passenger door and slid in. Her eyes were light brown and her hair was sun bleached almost blond with a print silk scarf tied around her forehead to hold the long strands down. She had on a cotton peasant blouse, faded jeans and sandals.

"Hi. Thanks for stopping."

"Where you going?"

"I don't know." She smiled. "Where you goin'?"

"Nowhere."

"Sounds perfect."

Then I knew, I just knew we were in 1950s. "You a friend of Jack's?"

"The writer? Sure am." She laughed. "You know Jack? He's so far out."

"I'm Ronnie." I said. "What's your name?"

"I don't believe in names, just call me Butterfly. Everyone else does."

"How do you know Jack?" I asked.

"Oh, we met when he and Dean were on a road trip to San Francisco. They stayed with me a couple of days out here in the desert." She laughed at the memory and added, "How do you know him?"

"Oh, I'm a big fan of his. I've read everything he ever wrote."

"Wrote some crazy shit, didn't he?" She laughed. "Listen, I have some good reefer if you wanna stop."

I pulled the car off the road next to a lone cactus. We sat on the RAV's cargo gate watching the sun go down. We smoked and laughed in the cool air until the night was black around us, except for a sky full of stars.

"Listen to this," I said, and quoted some of *On the Road* from memory.

She laughed and said, "Yeah, I remember him doing that."

I knew it was true. She had been with him for a space in the yesterday. I thought of a Kerouac poem that said in part, *In the endless past, In the endless present, In the endless future.*

When the air turned cold, I wrapped a blanket around us. She leaned against me and turned her head to kiss me. Her lips were light as the breeze blowing softly through the yucca bushes. We made love to the sound of a jazz piano over the radio. After a very long time we fell asleep in the back of the SUV.

Maybe we were there one night or possibly two. I'm not sure of anything except that I was completely lost in time with her.

And then she just disappeared.

"Wait!" I yelled to the empty desert. But she was gone. Like a butterfly.

I gassed the Toyota up near Needles and ate in a small café where truckers sat on stools at the counter with their ball caps pushed back on their forehead. Most of the caps had Freightliner or Peterbilt embroidered on the front. They were long haulers who knew the road ahead was a hard one. So, they flirted with the waitress and ate apple pie with their coffee, ready for the Mojave Desert.

"Make sure you got a full tank and lots of water," they advised me, "and a good spare, 'cause that hot asphalt will blow your tires."

I thought of my father, standing by the garage door with his arms folded across his chest, giving me the same warning.

The old highway across the Mojave was painfully monotonous. Along the broken and faded road, through a

5

thin, dark screen, I saw old Ford pickups or one-ton farm trucks piled high with household goods. Distressed men with sweat stained hats stood beside them while their women looked on helpless and children played in the ditches. I knew they were visions of that old American heartbreak, Dust Bowl survivors trying to make it to California, the land of milk and honey, still living in the Parallel Universe.

The heat was almost unbearable, and I wasted precious fuel by turning up my A/C as Gus panted on the seat beside me, his tongue hanging out, dripping saliva. At the beginning of twilight, I drew a breath of relief when the signs for Barstow came into view.

To my right there seemed to be some kind of encampment, so I pulled over. There were several abandoned Army tents, a couple of broken-down cars with the hoods up or the tires flat, and a few discarded kitchen chairs. A man sat in one of them, his elbows on his knees and his face in his hands. I pulled a chair close to him and sat, leaning forward.

"It's no use," he said. "They don't want us here. The big farmers try to pay 10 cents an hour and the Los Angeles police stand in the road with shotguns to keep us out."

"Where's your family," I asked.

"Stayed behind. I got to get back to them some way."

"What's your name?" But I knew before he answered.

"William Brady. From down by Tulsa."

I wanted to tell him it would be all right, that his children would be the greatest generation we had known and that his grandchildren would have a good life because of him and his courage. But he faded away into the twilight.

The next day, Gus and I drove to the base of the mountains. I knew that on the other side was the most beautiful farmland in the entire world. The Joad family had found it. Over 200,000 displaced families had found it and a new life.

I picked up the hardback copies of Steinbeck and Kerouac and kissed them, saying thank you for the glorious adventure into yesterday on Route 66.

 Nan Mahon is an award-winning journalist and novelist. Her works include *Blind Buddy and MoJo's Blues Band*, *Junkyard Blues*, and *Pink Pearls and Irish Whiskey*. Her short stories appear in several Capitol Crimes and other anthologies.

She has written and produced four large musical productions for the city of Elk Grove, CA. As a writer, band agent and theater producer, she has learned a sense of the artist's struggle and tells those stories. But, she also reaches back to her childhood for tales of struggle, as in her family anthology *Hard Times and Honeysuckle*.

Often gritty, her work gives voice to the disenfranchised and people living on the fringe of society.

THE TEENAGE QUEST
ELAINE FABER

I grew up in Sebastopol, California, a small town with one stoplight, and the only town in California where a train still daily ran down the middle of Main Street. In 1961, I was a senior in high school, drove a hot 1956 Plymouth, and was madly in love.

My task one Friday afternoon was to pick up Grandma after school and bring her home for the weekend. As I pulled into Grandma's driveway, she was waiting on the porch. We loaded Grandma's overnight bag, purse and a chocolate cake onto the back seat of my Plymouth and headed for home. Grandma chatted nonstop about raspberry bushes and moved straight on to canned pickles. It didn't matter that much to me. I pretty much ignored what she was saying, anyway. I was thinking about Lee, the gorgeous, hunky, tall, dark and handsome boy – the current object of my affection, who worked for my dad.

On Friday afternoons, after work, Lee came to the house to pick up his paycheck and always asked me if I wanted to go to the movies that night. More importantly, he'd be at my house about the time we'd arrived home. That's when Grandma spoke the fatal words. "Do you think we could stop at the drug store, dear? I need to pick up a few things."

My heart sank. "Grandma, we really don't have time. It's very important that I get home early tonight."

"Now, dear," she said in a tone of voice that only grandmas can use, "I'll only be a minute, and you know I don't get into town that often."

How do you argue with Grandma? I'd perfectly calculated my timetable. School let out at three-thirty. Pick up Grandma at four, home by five, and a movie date with

Lee locked in by six PM. And now Grandma wanted to stop at the drug store?

I parked Plymouth about a block away from the drug store, located between an ice cream parlor and a real estate office.

Grandma moved in slow motion from the parked car to the drug store, ambled through the aisle to select her purchases, and finally got up to the check-out counter. That's when we lost control.

The clerk's register tape broke. While fixing the tape, the phone rang and she had to read off the entire list of this week's sale items. The customer ahead of us bought a toilet brush without a price tag and the clerk had to find one correctly marked. The customer rejected the brush when she saw that it cost $1.52.

I wrung my hands, rocking first on one foot and then the other, watching the clock tick away the precious minutes toward five o'clock. Finally, it was our turn to pay. Just as I saw light at the end of the tunnel, my hopes shattered like spit hitting a hot griddle.

Grandma's hemorrhoid cream had a price tag, but the clerk had to look up the price on her enema bag. Her total purchase was $6.87. She licked her thumb and counted out six one-dollar bills. She then carefully placed two quarters, three dimes and seven pennies, one at a time on the counter, calling the total as she added each coin. "Six dollars and fifty cents, six dollars and sixty cents, seventy cents, eighty cents, eighty-one, eighty-two..." I was ready to scream by the time she got to six dollars and eighty- seven cents.

We returned to the car, in slow motion. Plymouth was well beyond the speed limit when we reached the highway outside of Sebastopol at five-fifteen PM. and my worst nightmare became reality. We passed Lee's little gray car. He casually lifted his hand and waved. His little foreign car appeared in my rear-view mirror, regrettably, disappearing down the road.

"Damn. We're too late," I screamed. "I knew we would be late. There he goes into town. I missed him!"

Grandma twisted to look over her shoulder at the cars headed the other way. "Who did we miss, dear?" My heart constricted. I couldn't breathe. The horrible truth pounded through my brain. I will have no date tonight. I slammed my fist on the steering wheel and gunned the engine.

"What's the matter, dear? Who was that? Should you be driving so fast? I'm getting dizzy. And, you really shouldn't say damn. A lady never swears. When I get really mad, I say bulldog! It's much more ladylike!"

I had to confess the reason for my unladylike outburst. "It's Lee, Daddy's new employee. He comes to the house every Friday afternoon for his paycheck and then he asks me out to a movie."

"Well, I swan! Why doesn't the young man call you on the phone before Friday night?"

"He knows I'll be there when he gets his paycheck. Now I've missed him, and I won't have a date tonight." My foot pressed the gas pedal in proportion to my frustration. Plymouth leaped to my command. Her tires squealed as we rounded the corner of my street, turned into my driveway, and skidded to a stop.

"Grandma, this is serious. No movie, no popcorn, no making out in the back seat!" Did I say that out loud? "Never mind! He's probably thinking about some other girl right this minute." I was frantically thinking how to save the desperate situation.

Grandma leaned into the car, gathering her belongings. She picked up her sweater, her purse and her packages. "Now where did I put that thing? Oh, there it is." She picked up the cake she had baked and laid down her overnight bag. The seconds ticked by. "No, that's not it." She set her purse down, and picked up something else. What could I do? He was getting away. Every second that passed, Lee was getting farther from my grasp.

"Get out! Get out! Get out!" I screamed, reaching for the door. "I'll bring your stuff in later!" I slammed the door, nearly catching Grandma's fingers as she reached for the chocolate cake. Her mouth dropped open. "Well, I shaw!"

I slammed Plymouth in reverse. Her tires spun, pitching

gravel in all directions until the wheels caught the asphalt. Plymouth's gears shrieked. As though she understood my teenage plight, she streaked down the road, where my heart's desire had disappeared. Mercifully, the highway didn't have a car on it. Plymouth lunged forward, 60, 70, 80, 90 miles an hour. At 90 mph, her front end shook and rattled and the steering wheel vibrated violently beneath my hands. I had to slow down to 85 mph.

Within several minutes, we were at the city limits, and I slowed the car to a mere 50 mph. Lee was NOT getting away!

Sebastopol is a small town with a single intersection and one traffic light. The traffic light, designed in the 1920s, when Model Ts shared the street with horses and carriages, had worked in my favor. It allowed pedestrians to cross the crosswalk, and then one or two cars to make a left turn onto the main street, and one or two cars to go either straight ahead or turn right. At five o'clock on a Friday night, it can take a while to get through the intersection. Several blocks ahead, I saw Lee's dilapidated little car stopped, about six cars back from the traffic light.

It had given me time to throw Grandma out of the car and return the mile to town where Lee sat stuck at the light, waiting to make a right turn. I thanked the long-dead City Fathers who had ignored their citizens' pleas to replace the antiquated traffic light on the only intersection in town, with a modern turning lane.

I made a quick right turn to circle the block, skirted through the parking lot behind the donut shop, and turned left into the alley next to the Chinese Restaurant. I swung right onto Main Street, placing me a good block beyond the antiquated traffic light where my intended still awaited his chance to make a right-hand turn. I raced up the hill on the outskirts of town, now several blocks ahead of my quarry, and parked in front of the Dairy Queen. A thin wisp of steam rose through the cracks around Plymouth's shivering hood.

After a touch of lipstick, and running a comb through my ponytail, it took about a minute and a half for Lee's rusty little car to chug into view. Ah, the glories of sweet success and anticipation.

Lee passed my car, and glanced toward Plymouth. I innocently waggled several fingers in his direction as he passed by. His head whipped around. He turned at the next corner and returned, where I waited, a tantalizing smile on my innocent, virginal, hopefully enticing face. Lee passed his hand over his incredulous face. "Didn't I pass you on the highway going the opposite direction, not ten minutes ago?" He pointed westward toward Santa Rosa.

"Yes, I believe you did," I said, looking alluringly innocent, as only a 17-year-old girl in love can look, having plotted, pursued, and run her unsuspecting prey to ground.

"How could you possibly be on this side of town? You never passed me on the road."

"I took a shortcut." I said, now coyly batting my eyelashes.

"But, how did you get through the traffic light? There's only one street through town."

"I didn't go through the traffic light," I said.

He glanced into the passenger seat. "I thought you had someone else in the car."

"That was just Grandma. I dropped her off at home before I came back into town."

Lee shook his head. It was a mystery beyond his paygrade.

In truth, I was blessed with good luck, a better knowledge of the small town than he had, and an overwhelming desire to reach my objective. I was also blessed with an antiquated traffic light, and armed with a hot 1956 Plymouth.

Guys really don't stand a chance. There are few forces in the world that compare to the hormones of an adolescent female with her sights on a man. A hurricane, an avalanche, a tsunami, a hurtling train, or a speeding bullet, don't hold a candle to the cunning, plotting, conniving, ruthless determination of a teenage girl in love.

Grandma forgave me, made another batch of pickles, and came for dinner the next Friday night. Daddy picked her up after work.

Well, to finish the story, I got my movie date that eventful night, and fifty-eight years later, I've still got that gorgeous, hunky, tall, dark and handsome guy, and he's still the current object of my affection.

Elaine Faber lives in Northern California. She is a member of Sisters in Crime, Cat Writers Association, and Northern California Publishers and Authors. She volunteers at the Elk Grove American Cancer Society Discovery Shop. Elaine's award-winning cozy cat mystery novels and humorous WWII adventure novels are listed below. Her short stories have also appeared in multiple anthologies. Elaine enjoys helping other writers and leads a writer's critique group in Sacramento.

Published novels:

Black Cat's Legacy
Black Cat and the Lethal Lawyer
Black Cat and the Accidental Angel
Black Cat and the Secret in Dewey's Diary
Mrs. Odboddy Hometown Patriot
Mrs. Odboddy Undercover Courier
Mrs. Odboddy And Then There was a Tiger
All Things Cat
The Spirit Woman of Lockleer Mountain
http:www.Elaine.Faber@mindcandymsteries.com (website)

THE GLASS HOUSE

SUSAN BETH FURST

On December 7, 1893, Phipps Conservatory and Botanical Gardens opened its doors to the public. The beautiful Victorian glasshouse built by steel magnate and philanthropist Henry Phipps Jr., was a gift to the people of Pittsburgh. It was just a hop, skip, and a jump from my great-great-grandmother's house in Bloomfield.

Every Easter Sunday, my sisters and I piled into the family station wagon for the long ride to Bloomfield. Mom would balance two lilies and the homemade coconut bunny cake on her lap as Dad took the scenic route through the cemetery. We would stop to pick Grandma up and then drive over the bridge to the Spring Flower Show at Phipps. Pap would stay home to watch the ham and the jellybeans.

Phipps Conservatory was my favorite place in the world, especially at Easter. The Sunken Garden Room was like a fashion show with all the colors of spring exploding in a kaleidoscope of daffodils, tulips, and hyacinths. Baskets of hydrangeas swung from the glass ceilings, and the sound of water splashed from the twin fountains. All the women in their posh pastel dresses and beribboned bonnets couldn't hold a candle to the Easter lilies.

Once, there was a blizzard. My sisters and I shivered in our new spring coats and hats as the snow piled up around us, frosting the Conservatory dome like a giant Easter cupcake. We took refuge in the Desert Room, where the old heating pipe hissed like a snake. My sisters stood next to the cacti and the fat succulents. I stayed on the concrete path far away from those beady-eyed mice in the agaves.

In 1898 Phipps Conservatory hosted the Triennial Conclave of the Knights Templar. I found the photograph in the gift shop. A lady named Angie Means was standing on a giant lily pad in the lake in the Victoria Room. She looked like a ghostly princess in her long white dress and dark hair. I wondered if she fell in and if the knights could swim with all that armor.

The Orchid Room always took my breath away, like the perfume from Murphy's 5 and 10 that we would buy Grandma for Christmas. Spanish moss and orchids would dangle from the trees like Santa's beard as goldfish skimmed the surface of the water below. Mounds of copper pennies would glint in the sunlight, and I would toss mine in. My wishes never came true. I'm not sure about the fish.

On a clear day, the outdoor ponds were full of blue sky and water lilies. Sometimes, my sisters and I would take off our shoes and dip our toes in the cloud's reflections, scattering them across the water. And when it was time to leave, we would sit on the benches beneath the flowering trees to wait for Dad to beep the horn.

Back at Grandma's house, we would eat ham, scalloped potatoes, and what was left of the jellybeans. Pap blamed Pastor Fattman's wife, who was known to have a bit of a sweet tooth. After dinner, he would get out the carving knife and slice the dark-chocolate fruit and nut egg from Yetter's. It was Grandma's favorite. Fortunately, for the bunny cake, none of us ever had any room left for dessert.

For over 125 years, Pittsburghers and people from around the world have enjoyed Phipps Conservatory's Spring and Fall Flower Shows. Six generations of my family have been there: my great-great-grandmother Jenny, her daughter Tressa, my grandmother Fern, my mother Betty Lou, my daughter Rachael, and me. Soon it will be seven! I plan to take my two granddaughters, Eliana and Madeline, in the spring. We will all pile in the back of the SUV. I'll hold the homemade coconut bunny cake on my lap, Pop-Pop will take the scenic route through the cemetery, and Pap will stay home to watch the jellybeans.

Susan Beth Furst is an award-winning children's picture book author and Japanese short-form poet. She has published three haiku collections: *Souvenir Shop, Road to Utopia,* and *Neon Snow.* Susan's books for children include *The Amazing Glass House* and *The Hole in My Haiku.* Susan was chosen to read her haibun, *Babylon,* for the David Labkovski Project's 2021 Holocaust Remembrance Day Commemoration Program. You can view the commemoration program and journal at davidlabkovskiproject.org. Susan lives in Fishersville, Virginia, located in the beautiful Shenandoah Valley. You can also find Susan and her books at PaperWhistlePress.com.

A LOT TO LEARN

BOBBIE FITE

In 2012, my sweetheart and I bought a sixteen-foot-long travel trailer. I'd been camping before, of course, but had never ventured far from home without a detailed travel plan or a tour guide. I was a little apprehensive about how this would work, but we were retired, we wanted to see the United States, and we had to be able to take our two little dogs with us. One does not leave dogs as cute and loveable as ours behind!

Because I am such a planner and despite Ernie's confidence, we created a step-by-step check sheet for setting up and breaking down camp in an RV park. We arranged for neighbors to pick up the mail, water the plants, and just keep an eye on things at home. Our campground reservations were made in advance for the duration of our week-long maiden journey down the east side of the Sierra Nevada Mountains, and everything went smoothly, just as Ernie knew it would. My fears quieted, we agreed that we were ready to take on a longer adventure.

A couple of months later, we packed up and headed toward Yellowstone National Park, with a number of well-researched stops along the way. You might have noticed that nowhere above have I referred to our experiences on the road as "trips." That is because, on our first night out, we were reminded that life doesn't always conform to our plans.

Two little dogs, two flexi-leashes (the kind that extend to sixteen feet), three ideas on which direction to take, and boom! I went down. Now that was a trip! Entirely the wrong kind of trip, so don't even mention the word around me! The doctor in the emergency room called my broken wrist a FOOSH (Fall on Out-Stretched Hand).

Okay, ice and Tylenol kept the pain at bay, and all we

had to do was find a hospital with an orthopedic department to apply a cast in a couple of days, once the swelling went down. No problem. We could continue with our planned vacation. Yellowstone beckoned, but first we saw Crater Lake and Bend, Oregon, then Craters of the Moon National Monument and Twin Falls in Idaho. A little over 150 miles short of our Yellowstone destination, we stopped in the emergency room at a hospital in Idaho Falls. New x-rays were taken and the orthopedic surgeon told us I would need a plate and screws to put my wrist back together. Did I want to have him do it on Monday? He had an opening in his schedule.

Uh, no. We'd go home for that, thank you. While I waited for copies of the x-rays and the written report, Ernie cancelled the next two weeks' worth of reservations, requesting refunds of deposits and repeating our sad story a dozen times. It took six days to get to Idaho Falls, only two to drive home, and no Yellowstone National Park. Not exactly what we'd had in mind, but it turns out that flexibility is an essential element for travel, and for wrists.

The surgery went well, the subsequent medical visits and physical therapy were overseen by my personal physician, the wrist healed, and we decided on a different strategy for future travels: plan ahead, but reserve as you go.

In April 2013, we set out again with our check list in hand, neighbors recruited, on-line banking set up, and reservations for only the first two nights. Our phones, tablets and laptop made it possible to pay our bills on line without missing a beat, make upcoming reservations, and handle the occasional crisis at home with email, text messages, and calls. Technology is amazing. Even if it is sometimes necessary to head to the park office or the local Starbucks to log on, in this day and age one can travel and still take care of business. Cool.

Onward now to our cross-country tour. We were gone for 165 days. We drove 21,000 miles through 39 states, and hit all four corners of the country. We had taken a map of the US and circled all the places with the people we wanted to visit and the sights we wanted to see. As we connected the dots, we called ahead a day or three before our expected arrival to make a camping reservation or confirm a visit with family or friends. It worked. The only exceptions to our new rule were advance reservations for a couple of national parks during holiday weekends. Thank goodness we had no more broken bones, but when something unexpected came up, as it always will, we were able to be flexible. Turns out that being flexible is mostly fun, not scary like I always believed.

Of course, there was that flat tire on the freeway that slowed us down, the tornado that closed the road, and mud so deep in one campground that we had to put plastic bags over our shoes and carry the dogs to the paved parking lot to do their business. Those dogs, by the way, get shaggy and stinky and do foolish things even (maybe especially) when you're away from home, making vet and groomer visits a necessity. Siblings, cousins, other family and friends we thought we'd just have lunch with, then move on down the road, said "Stay a while," and we did.

More than once we said, "Wow, look at that! Let's go see it!" Each time, the schedule changed, and almost always for the better.

We saw friends or relatives in California, Arizona, Texas, Kansas, Florida, Georgia, New Hampshire, Maine, Ohio, Wisconsin and Oregon. Some we had corresponded with regularly before beginning our travels and some we hadn't connected with for years. We had great visits, fun visits, interesting visits, and even a disappointing visit, but in every case, we were glad we'd reached out. In addition, we enjoyed meals, laughs and adventures with the new friends we made along the way.

If travel provides us with lessons and reminders, this one is to always make time for the people in our lives, especially the person you're traveling with. Dinner for two prepared on the barbeque and served with candlelight on a picnic table can be just as romantic as a meal at any fancy restaurant.

"I didn't know that!" has become a common

exclamation in our adventures. We have visited museums about trains and corn and the history of flight, to name just a few. In Pensacola, Florida, at the Naval Aviation Museum, four jets once flown by the Blue Angels are suspended from the ceiling of a conference or dining room, their wings nearly touching each other. Our guide told us he once brought a Blue Angles' pilot through on a tour and the pilot commented that the display was great, "but we fly closer together than that." Oh, my!

We visited all thirteen presidential libraries, plus a couple not run by the Department of Archives. What an experience. Almost every presidential library has a decision desk where they sit you down and you experience what it's like to gather the people you trust the most in the world when it comes to a topic like trade or jobs or health care or whatever, even war. Each of those trusted advisors presents you with information about a crisis in the making based on their own expertise and perspective. You must listen to them all, gather their wisdom, detect their biases, understand their reasoning, and make a decision. Right now. Not tomorrow. Being President of the United States is not for the faint of heart. As a visitor, you have the benefit of hindsight, but no president has had a fully functional crystal ball. We learned so much about the history of our country and the people who've held its highest office by spending time in these incredible museums that we recommend visits to fellow travelers all the time.

We have found that it is possible, even desirable, to get lost in a museum, both lost in the space when the collection wanders through several rooms on several floors like many an art or natural history museum, and lost in time while exploring a myriad of topics from ancient cultures to space flight. We like to read our way through the displays, and we also like to experience the wonders of our country.

The colorful lighting in Carlsbad Caverns turns stalactites and stalagmites into fanciful creatures. The Declaration of Independence is read from the steps of the courthouse in Williamsburg, Virginia, on the Fourth of July. Remembering it still gives us chills. The faces of presidents who represent the birth of our nation, its territorial expansion, the permanence of union, and the rights of the common man look out toward the future from a mountainside in South Dakota. Watching Old Faithful send water and steam skyward brings home the fact that you are standing in the crater of a massive volcano with power beyond our ability to comprehend. Across all the states, from vast deserts to thick forests to the highest mountains, nature has been our awesome companion.

Since that first excursion, we have twice traded in our older trailer for an upgrade. At twenty feet in length, the current model has a sofa, a bed we can walk around, an oven, and a shower worthy of the name. It is still the perfect size for almost any RV site, including those in our extraordinary state and national parks. During the past seven years, we have continued to explore this amazing country, ultimately visiting all fifty states and all of the bordering Canadian provinces and territories in our trailer. Well, there was one exception. Since the trailer doesn't float, we took a plane to Hawaii and rented a car.

In 2014, with our little house on the freeway, we spent three weeks exploring the southwest from the Grand Canyon (how do those mules make it safely down that treacherous trail?), to Arches National Park (rebar has to be the explanation for how those rocks stay in place), to Antelope Canyon where the swirling sand and water created some of nature's most beautiful sculptures.

We followed that the next year with two months traveling to and from Alaska. Glacier-fed Moraine Lake outside of Banff, Alberta, Canada, has water the blue-green color of a precious gem. The Top of the World highway from Dawson City to Chicken (the miners wanted to name the town after the local fowl, but couldn't spell Ptarmigan) wasn't nearly as terrifying as we had been led to believe. This part of the world only has two seasons: winter and road construction. That particular gravel road had been graded and repaired the year before. Whew!

Only 30% of the people who visit Denali National Park actually get to see Mount McKinley because the 20,308-

foot-tall mountain is generally shrouded in clouds, as it was the day we toured the park. But as we were driving south the next day, we caught a sparkle of white in the distance. "Did you see that? What was that? Could it be?" Yes, it was! Glacier covered, standing tall above the surrounding peaks, The Mountain posed for us and our cameras. The guide had said we would know it if we saw it. She was absolutely right, and it took our breath away.

We had planned this Alaska adventure around the ferry schedule between Skagway and Prince Rupert, with stops in Sitka, Juneau, and Ketchikan. Advanced reservations were a must, especially since our friend and neighbor from home was traveling along with us in his own trailer. Of course, when we went to board the ferry, we learned that a landslide had put the town of Sitka off limits. Change of plans. That's okay, we're flexible now, and the booking agent at the port was incredible, getting us where we needed to be when we needed to be there. Our Alaskan travels continued with salmon fishing (and eating), train rides, boat rides, an old-fashioned melodrama, hikes to watch glaciers calve, and a visit to a wonderful vet for a little emergency surgery to remove a thorn from a paw. That was immortalized by a t-shirt that says: *It's all fun and games until someone ends up in a cone*. What a summer that was!

We traveled across the country again in 2017 to see the states and provinces we had missed before and to visit again with friends and family. Music in Memphis, horses in Kentucky, a little waterfall in Niagara on the US-Canadian border (Oh, my!), and on and on. A month exploring Colorado another year, and six weeks to check out Glacier National Park the next, have kept us busy and on the road. We have photobooks filled with memories of the fabulous, and occasional less-than-wonderful-but-still-interesting, places we've been and the cherished people we've visited. We won't stop now, because there is always something new to see. The biggest lesson we've learned throughout our travels is simple: Go! It's worth it.

Bobbie Fite lives outside of Sacramento, California. This is her fourth story to appear in an NCPA Anthology. She has written three novels. In her first novel, Lauren's *NIGHTMARES* may be more than just bad dreams. She could be witnessing actual crimes. What happens if the murderer finds out she's helping the police? In her historical novel, *SUNSHINE AND THE BOUNTY HUNTER*, the title character has a bright smile, but no memory of her past or why she was riding across the Wyoming prairie alone. Was she riding for help, running away or after something else entirely? Finally, *STORM DAMAGE* takes place two days before Christmas when the roof of a busy shopping mall collapses. Buried in the debris are a young widow, a frustrated cop, a displaced great-grandmother and an abandoned child. They could wait for rescue, but buried with them is a killer with a great deal to lose. For more information, visit Bobbie's website: www.bobbiefite.com

THE GOLDEN DREAM

JACKIE ALCALDE MARR

Angelina pulled the invitation out of the gold-lined envelope and ran her fingers over the raised print. The box of invitations had arrived just before she and Daniel jumped in the car for their mini holiday, and they hadn't had a chance to review them together. "Mr. and Mrs. Steven Freeman and Mr. and Mrs. Johnathan Castle invite you to celebrate the marriage of their children, Angelina Sue Freeman and Daniel Wayne Castle…"

Smiling, she placed the invitation on the oak vanity, the one piece of furniture in their room at the historic Murphys hotel. She couldn't wait to build a life with Daniel. He was intelligent and warm, and he always made her laugh. And her parents liked him too. Her dad approved of Daniel right away. "An agricultural engineer with the Food & Drug Administration? It's a good, steady job, Lina."

Little did he know that Daniel hated that job. Instead, her fiancé dreamed of owning a vineyard and making his own wine. The thought of it made Angelina's stomach churn. They both needed steady jobs, and her salary as a high school teacher would not be enough for them to live on, let alone to start a family. She pushed aside the doubt that had nagged at her for weeks now and told herself, *He's just dreaming a bit. He'll grow out of it once we're married.*

"Whew! It's hot out there." Daniel stepped into the room and plopped onto his back on the four-poster bed. "What do you think of this place?"

"It's amazing, Hon. Did you see the Ulysses S Grant room a few doors down?" Angelina settled on the bed next to Daniel, both of them staring up at the ceiling.

"Yeah. I peeked in quickly. Wild, huh? And the bar downstairs? They say that's the original wood bar from

1856." He took her hand and brought it to his mouth for a quick kiss.

"Tell me again about your family and the property," Angelina asked.

He turned on his side, propped himself onto his elbow, and looked down at her with his light blue eyes. *He is such a handsome man,* she thought.

"So, it was my great, great grandparents who lived here during the famous gold rush! They had a little cabin on forty acres. It's always been in the family, and my dad inherited it when Grandpa passed. We used to come here a lot when I was a kid. Dad just wanted to check on the place. We'd drive by, but the house was a total wreck, so we never even got out of the car."

Angelina got up and went to the vanity with its large, oval mirror. "But I thought they started the hardware stores in the Bay Area way back in the 1800s?" Angelina asked him as she pulled her chestnut hair into a ponytail.

"Yeah, that's right," he said, coming up behind her. He wrapped his arms around her waist and smiled at their reflection in the mirror. "I think my great, great grandfather decided to move to Oakland when his wife died of a heart attack. Sadly, she never got to see the store. Grandpa loved that store, and my dad was the one who expanded the business. Once he opened the next couple of locations, they just got too busy. We didn't come here anymore. Shoot, we didn't do anything together anymore."

Angelina watched Daniel shift from excitement to disappointment. She put her hands on his and squeezed as she talked to their reflection. "Well, I've done my homework on Murphys. It was founded by the Murphy brothers, who operated a trading post here in 1848 to support the miners."

"I'm impressed," Daniel said. "Go on," and he kissed her neck lightly.

"Well, there was Albert Michelson – he was the first American to win the Nobel Prize for science. I think they named a school after him. And this guy, Mercer, he discovered huge caverns on his land grant. And then there were the bandits…"

"Can't you just imagine the energy in town? Everyone hoping to strike it rich!" Daniel put his phone in his pocket.

"Yeah…almost like you and your winery idea," Angelina couldn't help herself.

"That's different, Hon. I know we can make it a huge success," Daniel replied with confidence. "Speaking of which, let's walk the town and do some wine tasting. There are several tasting rooms within a stone's throw."

"Okay," said Angelina, "but maybe we should eat a little something first? I'm kinda hungry."

Daniel looked at his watch. "We only have an hour before the tasting rooms close. I'm sure they'll have something to munch on. Let's hit a couple of places, and then we can grab dinner. Okay?"

Angelina opened her makeup bag. "Okay. Let me spruce myself up a bit."

"You don't need any sprucing, Lina." Angelina saw Daniel's reflection in the mirror. He was looking at her adoringly. "You're prettier than a lilac in the spring."

Angelina rolled her eyes as she adjusted her ponytail.

* * *

"Just relax here, Lina. I'm going to get us some water, Okay?"

"Yep." That was all she could verbalize. She heard Daniel's voice and understood he wanted water, but she couldn't remember where they were. She closed her eyes and sat back in the chair.

She swallowed several times and rubbed her eyes, trying to focus. A large, framed photo on the wall grabbed her attention. She pulled herself out of the chair and stumbled the four steps across the small hotel lobby. She peered up at the photograph. The greys, tans, and creams of the sepia photo seemed to swirl in motion. She rubbed her eyes again and looked up at the photo. This time she saw the dirt street with buildings on either side and…yes, those were people standing on the side of the street, fuzzy and static. They were from a different time.

27

"Okay, Lina. I got us four bottles of water. I also got a box of those little wine tasting crackers, but you're going to need food at some point. C'mon, let's get you up to the room and into bed. Way too much wine for you!"

She heard all the words and felt Daniel put his arm around her waist. She let her head rest on his shoulder. She couldn't open her eyes. But she saw those people on the side of the dirt road, looking toward her, silent.

* * *

She grabbed the corner of the feather pillow and rolled onto her side. The sunlight was bright, and she squinted at the open window. White, lacey curtains blew into the room, a breeze bringing the smell of dust and smoke. *Someone must be barbequing.* Then the pain pounded in her temple as though someone was squeezing her head in a vice.

She ran her tongue across her lips – dry. She swallowed again and tasted the faint remnants of red wine. Then it came to her. *Did we visit three wine tasting rooms or four?* She felt behind her in the bed. Daniel wasn't there.

She swung her legs over the side of the bed. The room spun, and the white, lacey curtains fluttered wildly. She closed her eyes and waited a moment. Then she mustered the strength to stand up and move toward the vanity.

The large, oval mirror showed a young woman standing in her room. She turned around but no one was behind her. She turned back toward the mirror and pressed her fingers to her temples. *Gosh, there's a bowling ball inside my head.* The woman in the reflection was wearing a deep blue skirt, puffed full with folds. Her off-white cotton blouse had a row of tiny buttons running from the waist to the collar. Angelina touched the small cameo pin at the neckline. *Oh, my goodness...that's me!*

Okay, this is fun. I love these dreams that feel so real. I'll probably wake up any moment. She looked down at her feet. Scuffed black leather boots peeked out from under the heavy skirt. She remembered pulling her hair into a ponytail before she and Daniel went wine tasting. Now it was pulled back into a bun with stray hairs falling across her right cheek. Instinctively, she smoothed the hair against her head and tucked the loose strands into the bun. She smiled at herself in the mirror, waiting to wake up. *I think these are called lucid dreams. Well, since I'm not waking up yet, I might as well...*

A loud bang startled her. *Was that a gunshot?* Shouts came from downstairs in the bar, and it sounded like tables and chairs were being overturned. She ran down the stairs, holding the rail to steady herself, and stepped into the back of the bar. As she'd suspected, there was a brawl in full bloom.

"I ain't touched yer lousy gold dust, Harvey! But if you wan', I'll beat some out a' you anyway!" One man swung and the other ducked to avoid the fist.

Angelina stood dumbfounded. The people in the dimly lit bar were barely visible through the smoke that hung in the air. It was just like all the western movies she'd seen. *Well, of course it is*, she said to the stuffed moose head on the wall. *It's my own dream, now, isn't it?*

A woman came alongside her and scooped her arm through Angelina's, guiding her back out of the bar and into the lobby. "Careful there, deary. There's nothing to be done once Harvey and Sam have drunk their day's haul." The woman had a gentle but firm way about her. "C'mon. Let's head to the park. That's where all the fun is goin' on."

Angelina noticed the photo on the wall and the faces that still looked at her from the side of the dirt street.

Then they were in the bright sun, walking arm in arm. They were there! On that same dirt street! Angelina tried to relax. The woman patted Angelina's arm, "You're new in town, right? I don't believe we've met. I'm Catalina Castillo." She smiled and squeezed Angelina's arm just a bit.

"Pleased to meet you," Angelina replied, returning the smile. "I'm Angelina Freeman." *Just act natural, Lina. Go with it. How could it hurt?* She continued, picking up her confidence, "Yes. I just arrived in town." *Well, that is true.*

"Welcome to Murphys Diggins, Angelina. Don't let them rascals in the bar scare you off, now. We're a gentle bunch here. Most of the men are searching for their fortunes, and the women folk are just suffering through it." They continued down the road beside the hotel, and the community park came into view. "Where did you come from, deary?"

I came from 2021. No, that wouldn't go over well. "I'm from San Francisco."

"Oh! The big city! My husband and I have been thinking of picking up and moving there. We've been here a few years now, since '49. Came out just ahead of the crowds. Jay – that's my husband – he works for the Brainerd's. They own the hardware store at the end of town. Business is booming with picks and shovels, of course. But Jay and I – we'd like to open our own hardware store. We imagine folks really need building supplies out there in San Francisco. Tell me, please, do you think we're right?"

What did San Francisco look like in the 1850s? Angelina wondered. Her only reference point was the 1906 earthquake. Surely then they would need everything in the reconstruction effort. "Oh, I believe so. People always need building supplies, don't they? But nearby Oakland might be a better location." *More affordable, even then, I'm sure.* Home Depot and Lowes came to mind.

"Hmmm, Oakland. Well, it won't be for a year or two more. We're trying to save a bit of money. Got a young'un comin' along at the end of the year." She put her hand on her belly. "Where's your husband, deary? Is he finding his fortune as we speak?"

Angelina didn't know how to answer. "Oh, we're not quite married yet. We're planning to be wed in October. He's...he's in San Francisco, but he'll be joinin' me here soon." *Is that some sort of southern belle accent coming from my lips? Watch it, Lina. Don't overplay your role. Think: Little House on the Prairie.*

"Oh, that's wonderful. In the meantime, why don't you visit with us today? Wally Crump's little band is going to play some music for us, and Jay has our picnic all set up. There he is!" She waved over her head, and a tall man waved back before flicking a blanket in the air and settling it to the ground. A sweet grassy park hosted several families with their spreads, and a creek rumbled at the far edge. Two men were setting up a canopy on a wooden platform where another man was tuning the steel strings of a banjo.

"Jay, Honey, this is Miss Angelina. She's from San Francisco, and she's on her own today. So, I've invited her to join us."

"It's a pleasure to meet you, Miss Angelina." Jay put his hand on his heart and bowed his head respectfully. "Please sit," he gestured to the bright patchwork quilt. "We have plenty of food and a bottle of fine wine." Angelina's stomach turned.

"That's very kind of you, Mr. Castillo," she said as she knelt on the quilt, her thick skirt billowing around her.

"Oh, please call me Jay. And my wife is simply 'Lina."

"That's funny. My friends call me 'Lina' too," Angelina said, deciding that she really liked this young couple.

Catalina dug into the picnic basket and pulled out a loaf of brown bread and four apples. She brushed the back of her hand across her forehead, "My word, it's quite warm today. I feel I'm wilting."

"Oh, my Lina, you are as pretty as a lilac in the spring," said Jay as he reached over and squeezed her hand.

The words rang in Angelina's head. She remembered Daniel saying the same thing to her earlier that day…or was it yesterday? *Dreams are so funny. But I'm ready to wake up now. Daniel's going to get a kick out of this.*

She pinched her arm firmly. Then again, even harder. But she was still there, and Catalina handed her an apple. "Are you all right, Miss Lina?"

"Oh, yes, thank you." Angelina smiled as best she could even though panic was welling into her throat. She flashed through memories of time traveling stories – *Outlander, Timeline, The Time Traveler's Wife*. It couldn't possibly be that this vivid dream was not a dream at all. *No. No. You just had way too much wine on an empty stomach. You just need to sleep through this.*

Jay got up and said, "I'm going to help Wally with that tent." He kissed Catalina on the cheek and nodded to Angelina. His blue eyes sparkled brightly in contrast to his tan face.

Catalina watched him trot over to the stage, then turned to Angelina, "Tell me about your lucky fiancé, deary."

"Oh, well..." Angelina hesitated. "He's a very kind man...and handsome. And he makes me laugh."

"That's a mighty fine quality. After all, you'll be together the rest of your lives. It's good to find humor every day, and especially on the days that test your soul." Catalina handed Angelina a chunk of cheese. "Oh, my dear, I can see some doubt in your eyes. What is it?"

Angelina was surprised she'd revealed a trace of doubt. Did Daniel or her parents see the same thing in her eyes? "Well, it's just that he has such big dreams..." She looked down at the quilt as shame heated her cheeks. Then the words burst forward. "I want to support him, but I feel he should be pursuing a steady and secure job, rather than chasing these outlandish dreams that will probably amount to nothing."

A silence fell on the quilt until Catalina finally spoke. "My dear." She put her hand on Angelina's. "Look around you," she swept an open hand in front of her. "This town is full of men with outlandish dreams. There is time for them to find a sensible job, as they surely will – some much sooner than others. In the meantime, the gold fever has captured their hearts and compels them to keep trying. It gives them life." She took a bite of her cheese. "Goodness, sometimes I think it is the pursuit of the dream that is just as satisfying as finding a fine nugget. I suppose it's the same as when they're courting their girl. Right?" She smiled at Angelina.

She continued, "I know that Jay would love to pull a gold boulder from the ground." She winked at Angelina, "He's actually done pretty well, and I've squirreled away the gold he's found so far." She lowered her head and whispered with a little smile, "I've hidden those bits away in a coffee can under the hearth of our fireplace. He's happy he doesn't know where they are." She giggled. "And I'll support his dreams of the gold. It thrills him so. In the end, the real dream is to share a life together. Soon we'll build the life we truly want – opening our own mercantile – in

Oakland." She smiled and nodded with satisfaction.

Catalina's words stuck to Angelina like honey. Daniel glowed when he spoke of his dream winery.

*   *   *

"Lina! Lina, c'mon. Wake up!"

She opened her eyes as Daniel swept a lock of hair from her forehead. "There you are," he said, smiling at her. "You were totally out! I'm sorry, Hon, I should have made sure you had something to eat."

Angelina rubbed her eyes and sat up. Her head still felt heavy. "Daniel, you really need to do the winery," she said without thinking. The lacey curtains fluttered in the window, and she had an overwhelming sense of déjà vu. She cupped his cheek in her hand and said, "You won't believe the dream I just had."

*   *   *

It was a one-lane road that twisted its way around massive oak trees. "There it is," said Daniel as he pulled into a drive that was covered in knee-high weeds. All that remained of the home was one wall with a shattered window pane and half of a stone chimney.

"Wow. It's amazing. To think your great, great grandparents lived here..." Angelina stood beside the window.

"Yeah. They should have one of those historical markers, *Here stands the home of Joaquin and Catalina Castillo*," Daniel said with bravado.

"What? Why isn't his last name Castle, like yours?" Angelina asked, feeling a little uneasy.

"Well, his name was actually Joaquin Castillo. But around that time there was a gang of bandits known as the Five Joaquins. Your research probably mentioned Joaquin Murieta, right?"

"Yeah, I remember seeing that," she replied.

"I think that he didn't want to be known as a Joaquin.

33

So, he went by *Jay* back then. Dad said he changed his full name to Jason Castle when he moved himself to Oakland and opened the store."

Angelina's head swam with bits that nearly coalesced. Jay and Catalina. The scenes of her dream came into focus.

She stepped over broken boards to the stone fireplace. Several stones were scattered around it, having fallen from the chimney. She found the corner of the hearth and began picking at the rocks.

"Lina, what are you doing?" Daniel came up beside her.

She lifted one large stone and saw a dull red can buried beneath it. She dug around it with her hands and freed it from its tomb.

"What in the world? Lina, how did you know to dig for this?" Daniel took the can from her trembling hands.

The contents rattled as he shook it. He pried the lid off and tipped the contents into his palm. Several gold nuggets spilled over his hand and the sun made those left in his palm sparkle.

"Let me tell you about that dream," said Angelina.

 Jackie loves wine, nourishing old friendships, all things Spain, and the lessons of history. She is a lifelong learner and loves to pack her bag for adventure.

After a long corporate career as an organization development leader, Jackie became an independent consultant, trainer, and certified leadership/life coach. She created Evolutions Consulting Group to help individuals and groups achieve their goals while accentuating their core passions. She works with private, public, and non-profit organizations, as well as individuals who are creating fulfilling lives.

Jackie co-authored *Social Media At Work: How Networking Tools Propel Organizational Performance* (Jossey-Bass). She has been published in the Sacramento Business magazine, the Organization Development Journal, and several of NCPA's anthologies.

She's currently writing the story of her family's immigration from Spain through Hawaii to California. She lives in Folsom with her husband Jeff and their mischievous mutt, Quincy Noodlebutt.

BORN 100 YEARS TOO LATE

SHARON S DARROW

My three brothers were born 100 years too late, as illustrated by my favorite picture of them. Mike, Pat, and Jerry all had long, bushy hair, with a full beard and mustache. Dressed in Civil War uniforms, complete with holsters and guns, they were sitting at a saloon corner table with whiskey bottles, glasses and poker cards in front of them. Unlike some staged pictures in period costumes, they looked quite comfortable—every inch the dangerous soldiers they were portraying.

Perhaps it's a young man thing, but my brothers loved fighting. And I'm talking about full-blown fist fights. If they were outnumbered and outweighed, that just added to the fun.

One time they were in Mike's pickup truck, traveling on back roads on the way home. They were headed to Sacramento from somewhere in the Sierra Nevada mountains around Reno. Another old truck with three rough-looking guys approached from the opposite direction. Instead of minding their own business and letting the truck pass, Mike let loose with a loud wolf whistle. Sure enough, the other truck pulled a tight U-turn and followed my brothers to the next turnoff at the side of the road, tucked up against the steep hillside.

The doors burst open as soon as both vehicles stopped. Six young men in two groups of three, puffed up and posturing like bantam roosters, faced one another. The three facing my brothers were older and a little rougher looking—two of them waved knives in front of their bodies, while the third had a short chain wrapped around his right fist.

Unarmed except for his wit and his mouth, Mike yelled,

"What, you too chickenshit to fight with your bare hands?"

His strategy worked. The other three threw their weapons back into their truck and charged.

The fighting was hidden from the road by the parked trucks, so no one stopped and attempted to intervene. Of course, it's always possible that somebody might have stopped, then decided it was best to stay out of what was a well-matched fight, and drive on. In any event, no one interrupted the bare-knuckled brawl.

According to the story my brothers told me, the fight continued to a draw, stopping only when everybody was too tired to continue. All six idiots ended up with an assortment of swollen, scraped knuckles, bruises and black eyes, facial cuts and split lips. I have no idea of what the strangers told their families, but my brothers laughed and claimed that they'd had a great time.

As "big sister" I heard about many of my brothers' exploits, but was never sure how much to believe. As adults, they seemed to have toned down—at least I was no longer hearing about fist fights—but one day at the Sacramento International Airport, I learned that they hadn't changed at all.

Our grandmother, Lillie, was dying in a hospital in Hollister, Missouri. She was our birth-father's mom, and I hadn't seen her for many years. Mike had been visiting her and her husband for a week, but had to come back home to Sacramento. He called and told me that she'd asked me to come if I could. As a working mother of two little girls, it wouldn't be easy, but my husband helped me make the arrangements.

Our plan was for me to meet Mike at the airport when he returned, so we could talk before I left. Pat and Jerry had already planned to pick Mike up when he arrived, so the four of us would kill time together while waiting for my plane.

Our intention was simple—the four of us could have some quality time to catch up, since we hadn't been together alone to talk and reminisce for years. The boys chose a small cafe that served alcohol, and bought drinks. I'm the wild one of the bunch, so I opted for diet coke.

The "remember when" stories were wonderful and we laughed more than we had in years, right up until I glanced at my watch and saw that it was time for my plane to leave. We had counted on hearing flight announcements in the restaurant, but hadn't heard a thing. Much too late, we learned that the announcements weren't broadcast inside the little cafe.

I leaped up in a panic. "Oh my god, I'm going to miss my plane."

The boys jumped, looked at each other, and chorused "No way. You'll make it."

Mike grabbed my left arm, Jerry grabbed the right, and Pat picked up my suitcase and took off. Mike and Jerry lifted me off my feet and took off at a dead run after Pat and my luggage.

"Get out of the way, we're coming through!" They shouted and laughed all the way down the concourse to the boarding gate. The airport was full of people, but the loud warnings and the spectacle of me being carried between my brothers cleared a path through the crowd.

I was embarrassed down to my toes, but couldn't do anything since I was hanging in the air between them. The temptation to close my eyes was almost irresistible, but I feared that might be even worse. My feet didn't touch ground until we arrived at the desk to check in for my flight, where we found the airline attendant closing the door to the jetway.

I begged, I pleaded, I explained about how important it was to get to my destination before my grandmother passed away. Heart-felt tears at the thought of not being able to say goodbye to her slid down my face. All to no avail. The attendant was unmoved and refused to hold the plane for the five minutes it would have taken me to board.

His rigid attitude might have been influenced by the belligerent tone my brothers took, but nothing made any difference. His only concession was to book me on another flight scheduled for two hours later, with no penalties or extra fees. I gave up fighting about what I couldn't change, moved to the boarding area for the new flight, and prayed

I'd arrive in time. No restaurants this time. I parked myself in a chair near the gateway door and pulled out a book to read until flight time.

I thanked the boys for their help, and told them they might as well go on home. "I'll be fine, and I'll let you know when I arrive. When I see Lillie, I'll call Stan with an update, and he'll pass it on to you guys."

"We know you will, but we'll stick around just to make sure you get on the plane okay." Mike looked at Pat and Jerry as he spoke, and I sensed something was going on.

Sure enough, in seconds my brothers disappeared from sight. So much for keeping an eye on me. Just as well, it would be a lot more peaceful waiting alone. I did glimpse them every now and then. Oddly enough, it was always one of them alone, very focused, walking at a brisk pace.

They were focused, all right, steadfast and single-minded in their determination to make the attendant regret not letting me on the plane. And, of course, to have some fun at the same time.

For nearly two hours they terrorized that poor, snotty attendant. From his station at the gate desk, the attendant could watch all the foot traffic in the massive terminal. He could also see people coming down a wide escalator, folks exiting a bank of elevators, and people coming and going through glass doors located in a wall of windows on one side of the massive room. My brothers had a terrific time traveling all over the terminal with the attendant at the center of their attention. It didn't take long for the attendant's confidence to deflate as each appearance of one of them—from a new spot each time—rattled him more and more.

When the boys shared the story with me, they said they had a great time watching the attendant's face turn white each time one of the them made eye contact with him. They'd grin, point, and make threatening gestures before disappearing into the crowd—only to see the guy look more rattled whenever one of them appeared. Their entertainment ended when the wide-eyed attendant was escorted out of the building by a trio of tough-looking security guards, all the way to the parking garage.

One of the reasons the boys had such fun was the element of danger. There was always a possibility that they'd get caught, which would have carried a hefty penalty, much more severe than a fist fight on a mountain road. Drug laws were a lot different back then—and each one of my brothers had enough marijuana in their pockets to put them in jail or prison. Some fun!

Sharon Darrow is an entrepreneur, business owner, award winning author, public speaker, and expert in caring for neonatal orphan kittens.

Two of her books are about animal rescue, *Bottlekatz, A Complete Care Guide for Orphan Kittens* and *Faces of Rescue, Cats, Kittens and Great Danes.* Two are inspirational: a memoir titled *Hindsight to Insight, A Traditional to Metaphysical Memoir* and *Tom Flynn, Medium & Healer.* Her fifth non-fiction is a training manual about publishing, *Navigating the Publishing Maze, Self-Publishing 101.*

Sharon also writes historical fiction. *She Survives, Strive and Protect, Desperate Choices* and *Her Triumph* are the four books in the Laura's Dash series, inspired by her maternal grandmother. Sharon firmly believes that life just gets better and richer, the longer you live. Her personal motto is "Find harmony within, then all things are possible." Her website is https://www.sharonsdarrow.com, her publishing website is https://www.samatipress.com.

Email her at sharon@sharonsdarrow.com.

MY FIRST PET

LORNA GRIESS

For the first half of my career in the Army Nurse Corps, I enjoyed a life of travel and work. All of my possessions fit in my 1957 Volkswagen. The next assignment to anywhere was an adventure. Then, orders came to go to Ft. Polk, in the back woods of Louisiana.

Ft. Polk, in Army medical circles, was not exactly known as a prime assignment. It was an hour drive from the nearest shopping mall. It was a basic training base – hot and humid most of the year. My first impression was not good. As I pulled into a long drive, the only visible thing for as far as the eye could see was an old looking, WWII cantonment style hospital: a group of one-story wood-framed, sun-bleached buildings connected by long covered corridors. There were miles of corridors, none of which were at the same level.

Did not know at the time that those corridors would be in my future as evening and night supervisor.

After officially signing into the hospital and visiting the chief nurse, the priority became finding a place to live. Many people made suggestions and gave directions. There were not very many choices so the decision was made to move into a furnished apartment in the adjoining town of DeRidder. It was a nice new apartment building in the beginning rental stages. As the second person in the whole two-story building of fourteen apartments, second floor was a good option. Household goods were soon delivered and I happily started setting up a household, quickly establishing my routines for work and home. I did begin to notice a lot of bugs. The balcony had wasps; the storage closet, black widow spiders and large, inch and a half long, brown roaches. A serious sense of dread sent a shiver through my

42

body.

Getting to know people and making a few friends was a must at a new assignment. Any conversation, however it started, had the recurring themes of work, the roaches inhabiting the hospital and homes, and the persistent humidity and heat.

This was a small, community type hospital supporting a basic training post and a retired community. Most of the patients were young. Obstetrics did a thriving business. Geriatrics did not. Because of the long corridors the supervisory personnel used a golf cart to make rounds. It was fun riding up and down the uneven corridors. We did not surprise anyone because the golf carts shook the buildings attached to the ramps.

The night nurse, Mrs. D, knew I did not like roaches to the point of being afraid of them. Of note is that Mrs. D. was a short, oversized grandmother with a wonderful sense of humor. When she entered the building at 10:45 PM, I could hear her clump or crunch her way to the nursing office. Smiling, she would poke her head in the door and say, "It's safe to leave now, I stepped on all the critters on my way in." Sure enough, it looked like a war zone when I left.

One day a friend, another nurse, stopped me in the hallway and said, "You need a cat, and I have just the one."

I said, "No, I don't need a cat."

She added, "Because you don't have a pet, you need one." She continued to tell me that she had a dog, a puppy. She was driving down a country road a few days ago and saw a stray cat, a Siamese, that had been dumped. She had looked for the owner without success and she couldn't keep it because her puppy wouldn't leave it alone.

If the cat was under the bed the puppy would lie on its side and scoot under to get her. The cat was terrified. That got me. Reluctantly, I agreed to go and look. It was a cute cat. A young, female, Seal Point Siamese with wonderful, expressive eyes. The cat immediately crawled up in my lap and sat staring at me.

What to do? The cat was mine. This required a trip to the store for a carrier, food and litter supplies. A friend

43

helped me get her home.

Home with the cat, I opened the door the usual way – carefully to let the roaches skitter away before stepping in. After putting the carrier down in the hallway, and opening the door to let the cat out, amazingly, her first move was to dart after and kill a roach.

Then she hid under the bed.

Unbelievable! The perfect roommate. A wonderful and useful cat. I loved that cat. In about a week she got used to her new, non-threatening surroundings and became friendly, loveable and playful. My life changed with the responsibility for caring for something other than myself.

For the rest of my stay at Ft Polk, roaches were not an issue – until it was time to leave.

Reassignment orders came for the hospital in San Francisco. Unbelievable good luck, it was in California, close to home. My last day in the apartment, I got up to make coffee and there was a roach swimming around in the left-over coffee in the drip style coffee pot. The cat must have chased it until it lost its balance and fell into the pot.

The whole mess went down the garbage disposal with its blades spinning. Then the pot went in the trash. I really hated roaches, and made sure the packers did not pack any in my boxes.

Over time, I grew to love cats. There has been a cat or two in my house until last September when my last one died at age 16. I miss her a lot. When it's time to look for a replacement, preference will go to a healthy older cat that somebody had to give up because of illness or death.

Kittens are cute and fun but the comfort and wisdom of an older cat is immeasurable.

A second-generation native Californian, Lorna graduated from high school and nursing school in Sacramento. Her first job was staff nurse at the Woodland Clinic in Woodland. Restless, she joined the Navy Nurse Corps with an assignment in Newport, RI, in time for the Cuban Crisis in the early 60s. After two years she returned to civilian life and moved to New York City because the World's Fair was coming. She found a job at Cornell Medical Center on the east side of Manhattan. Missing military life, and with the escalation of the conflict in Vietnam, she rejoined the military, this time, the Army Nurse Corps with a guaranteed assignment to Vietnam. She found a home

The Army became a career. After serving in a MASH unit in Vietnam, her assignments took her to Germany and all parts of this country. She worked her way through staff nurse, head nurse jobs in intensive care and oncology. Then had supervisory roles in large hospitals. She retired after 28 years of service as a full colonel, chief, Department of Nursing at Letterman Army Medical Center on the Presidio in San Francisco. The hospital closed shortly after she retired in 1990.

Retirement opened up a new world of opportunities. She worked as a nurse for a short time and then fully retired from nursing. She was a veterans advocate at the state capitol for nine years representing the Military Officer's Association. A lifelong hobby photographer, she became an artist. Painting with oils she now looks for pictures to paint in her large stash of old photographs. She has written a book about her year in Vietnam in a MASH Unit called "MASH Vietnam." She now stays busy with volunteer work. Much of which is with her church: artwork, crafts, and community outreaches such as Saturday Community Meals to feed the homeless and Sandwiches in the Park.

A VISIT TO PELE'S TEMPLE

TOM KANDO

When we vacation in Hawaii, with family and/or friends, we usually avoid the hustle and bustle of Honolulu. To be sure, even parts of the other islands such as Maui are highly developed by now.

However, Maui also has one of the world's most awesome volcanoes, and inside its crater, one of the world's most desolate, lonely, remote, spectacularly beautiful and pristine places.

Pele is the Hawaiian goddess of fire and volcanoes. Haleakala is the 10,000-foot volcano which occupies the largest part of the island. Dormant since 1750, this majestic mountain is truly Pele's temple.

The Haleakala crater is one of the world's largest. It has a circumference of 31 miles. It is large enough to contain all of Manhattan. To descend into it, cross it and get out of it on the other side requires a twenty-two-mile hike. Shaped somewhat like a horseshoe, the wall of the crater has a gap in the rear towards the southwestern shore of Maui. Thus, one can hike through the entire crater, beginning at the top, above 10,000 feet, follow the sliding sands trail all the way through the Kaupo gap, and end at sea level on the other side of the island two days later.

I first conceived of dragging my daughters through this surrealistic landscape back in the late 1980s, when they were only nine and eleven years old.

Here we were in the midst of luxury hotels and condominiums at Kaanapali Beach, the height of comfort. In the distance I could see the immense mountain, and I knew that less than fifty miles away there was an absolutely unspoiled, virgin, vacant no-man's land rarely visited even by park rangers. I wanted to experience the contrast and show it to my kids – a contrast as sharp as that between Las Vegas and Death Valley, or Los Angeles and the bottom of the Grand Canyon.

We managed to cross the crater that year in two days. We carried our backpacks, tent, food and water for two days. Eleven-year-old Danielle suffered from dehydration; little nine-year-old Leah's blisters turned into a bloody mess. There were many tears and arguments. At times the girls refused to continue, but we had no choice. Going back up would have been far more difficult than continuing the descent. Finally, after two days, we came out, exhausted, haggard, but victorious. What an adventure!

Since then, this trek has become sort of a family tradition. The girls and I have done it several more times. We also managed to convince some of our American and European friends and relatives to share this memorable experience with us, sometimes doing this incredible two-day 10,000-foot descent as a group of six or eight people. For this, some of them are eternally grateful to me, while others will never speak to me again. I feel that these Kando family treks qualify for the Guinness Book of Records.

We have always done the hike in two days. There is no way that you and your children can hike the 22 miles of arduous, mountainous trail, fully loaded, in less than that. But the trip is no longer traumatic. Now it is merely a fine, tough, beautiful, marvelous experience.

The problem with crossing Haleakala is partly logistical: you have to start on top at more than 10,000 feet, so someone must drop you off there with all your equipment. Then two days later someone has to pick you up on the other side of the island, well over 100 miles of twisted road from your hotel.

The designated driver has always been my wife, Anita. So, on the day of the drop-off, she drives us up to the top of Haleakala, which is a five-hour, 110-mile roundtrip from our hotel on Kaanapali Beach.

Then, on the evening of the second day, Anita has to pick us up at the other end. And this is complicated. You see, the end of the trail is a place on the map marked

"Kaupo." (Hence the name "Kaupo Gap" to designate the gigantic breach in the crater's wall at the southern end, through which you hike on your way down.)

You'd think that this is a village, but it is only a ramshackle grocery store that is open for the local Hawaiian cowpokes every day from noon till two. It is the most isolated and poetic place imaginable. There is no paved road to the Kaupo grocery store. The closest you can get to it with your rental car is to take the famous 65-mile incredibly curvy and narrow road to Hana, and then continue for another ten miles to the Seven Sacred Pools.

That's as far as Anita can drive.

Beyond that, the road is a rocky, sometimes muddy mess, often washed out by torrential rain. You usually don't have four-wheel drive and you are not insured since the rental companies forbid you to drive there. When Anita comes to pick us up, she will end up driving for a total of another six hours, covering 180 miles to get us and drive us back to the Kaanapali Marriott.

But when we reach the end of the trail at Kaupo, we are still eight miles away from her. So, we improvise. Some years, we manage to hitch a ride in a local Hawaiian rancher's jeep or truck. Sometimes they do it for a modest payment. Sometimes they don't accept any money. Some years we have to walk for several more grueling miles, beyond the twenty-two miles we just covered.

All in all, my wonderful wife has to be our chauffeur for a total of eleven hours and drive three hundred tortuous and dizzying miles over a period of two days to drop us off and pick us up.

*   *   *

So now for the main event - the hike:

Basically, it consists of crossing the entire national park, and then some. On the second day, we exit the park and go through many miles of ranch land, gradually descending the slopes of Haleakala. Here, finding our way becomes a real challenge, as the trail often disappears.

Before starting the hike on the first morning we must register at National Park Headquarters. If we don't come out at the appointed time and place, they come looking for us with helicopters.

Then the hike begins. It consists of two days of a grueling, nonstop descent. Twenty-two miles, a 10,000-foot vertical drop, 70,000 downward steps. We carry our backpacks, tent, and all the food and water needed by the entire group for two days. There's no water anywhere inside the crater, except at the campground, ten miles away. The pounding on our quadriceps is something which will cripple us and from which we will need a week to recover.

At the outset, the trail is well marked, because of a total absence of vegetation. Not only are we above the tree line, but there's absolutely no other growth either. Not even flies. The landscape is totally lunar.

Gradually, the trail becomes more tortuous. As we descend into an increasingly tropical environment, we come across some vegetation, and at times the trail disappears or becomes difficult to negotiate.

A major problem is watching our steps. The trail is extremely rocky and uneven, carved out of lava in most places.

My foot folds underneath me several times, but fortunately nothing gets sprained or broken. Were that to happen to any of us, we would have to be rescued by the National Park Service. But I have no idea how we would call for help, as there is zero iPhone reception inside the gigantic crater.

By late afternoon, we have covered the ten miles getting us to the Paliku campground, one of only two in the entire national park. We pitch our tent at 6,500 feet elevation. There isn't another soul, not another tent, no one, just us and the Nene birds – the indigenous Hawaiian geese which seem quite curious and unafraid of us.

Paliku is fine during the sunny afternoon. But the weather turns quickly at six and a half thousand feet inside a volcano. Often, sunset brings in moist clouds, and we get drenched. On our first trip, the night was a nightmare. Water seeped into the tent, we were lying in puddles of water, soaked to the bone, huddled together to keep as warm as possible. I recall not being able to sleep one single solitary second, looking at my watch every half hour, praying for the sun to come up.

But now, as it begins to lighten up, we start moving about, shivering, suffering, clumsily collecting ourselves for the remainder of the trip. The following year the rain was milder, but we were still cold and uncomfortable. Getting up at Paliku, one is *always* cold, tired and miserable.

Yet, the beauty is so awesome, the surroundings so unlike anything else on earth, that one's spirits cannot sag. Sometimes, when the night sky is clear, the view of the stars and the milky way is unimaginably clear and gorgeous (the observatory on top of Haleakala is one of the world's best). In the morning, when you get out of your tent, you look up at the crater's gigantic walls surrounding you, and the cinder cones in the distance. At least twenty such mini-volcanoes dot the floor of the giant crater itself. Each of these cinder cones is itself several hundred feet high, but is dwarfed by the gargantuan walls of Haleakala, which are measured in the thousands of feet. We have a quick breakfast, pack up in the drizzle and resume our hike – alone in our splendid isolation, not having seen or heard a soul since yesterday morning.

For the first couple of hours, we are dressed for rain and cold. But soon the clouds dissipate, the rain stops, the sun begins to beat down upon us, and all the time we are descending towards ever lower, more tropical and jungle-like conditions.

Soon we long for the freezing weather of the previous night. Now the opposite discomfort takes over. We begin to sweat, to thirst, to pant. On our first trip, the temperature ranged from the 30s to the 90s.

We are now passing through the Kaupo gap. This is where the walls of the crater are interrupted. On both sides, walls rise several thousand feet. The gap is several miles wide. It takes us hours to hike through this part.

We have finally begun to see the ocean - far down in the distance. Eventually, we reach the exit of the national park. From here on, the Kaupo trail meanders through wide open range, tribal ranch land owned by the Hawaiians. The vegetation becomes incredibly lush. The trail disappears. We get lost and have to back up to find our way again. We see some bovine creatures in the distance. Hopefully cows, not bulls; hopefully friendly. Their horns don't look very friendly. We circle around them rather than cross paths with them. We are hot, in pain, thirsty, with barely any water left. The coast, our destination, seems to recede forever. An endless descent, it seems.

It's 3 PM already. We are supposed to meet Anita at 6, by the Seven Sacred Pools. Can we make it? She is to wait until dark, and only alert the authorities after dark, if we don't show up. Well, that gives us several more hours.

Finally, by about 5, we discern the Kaupo general store. Hooray! We made it! Haggard, disheveled, filthy, smelly, but happy. That's how we present ourselves to the few locals who are sitting around, sipping drinks inside the grocery store. Curiously, the store is open this time, even though it's after 2.

We ask the store owner for water, and he gives us some. Then we must face the next problem: how to cover the remaining eight miles to the rendezvous point by the Seven Sacred Pools, where the drivable road begins. I wave a $20 bill: "Anyone willing to drive us out of here? You guys have trucks and jeeps, four-wheel-drive. Look at my poor tired girls. Please!"

Most of the times we have done Haleakala, we have managed to hitch a ride out of Kaupo. This time, again, a friendly Hawaiian volunteers to drive us out. His name is Roland. He tells me to stop waving my money in his face. Hawaiians don't do things for the money. He drives us out because he likes to.

The trail out is a narrow, twisting cliffhanger. It takes Roland nearly an hour to drop us off at the Seven Sacred Pools because, on the way, he insists on stopping at his house and proudly showing it to us, overlooking the ocean hundreds of feet below. A magnificent view of cliffs, beaches, and the volcano. I'm keenly aware of the immense contrast between Roland's lifestyle and ours. Kaupo is so remote, so inaccessible, so beautiful. Roland tells us that much of the year, basic necessities and medical help are only available by helicopter.

When we finally meet up with Anita in the parking lot at the Seven Sacred Pools, she has been fretting. She arrived there well ahead of our appointed time, with an ice chest full of cold drinks and chilled mangoes, pineapple and passion fruit. It's after 6 PM. She has already shared her worries with a park ranger on duty there. But everything is fine. We devour the contents of the ice chest and dive into one of the seven pools, washing off two days of sweat, dust and fatigue.

Then it's back to the luxury hotel on Kaanapali Beach, three hours away via the harrowingly twisted Hana Road. A few days later, sadly, we return home to the mainland.

So, you see, to us Maui isn't just luxury beaches, luaus and tourist attractions. Above all it is Pele's Temple – the magnificent, silent, virgin vastness of Haleakala to which we have returned time after time.

Tom Kando, PhD, grew up in World War II Europe, spending his formative years in Paris and Amsterdam. At eighteen, he came to America as a lonely immigrant and a Fulbright student. He became a professor at major universities, taught in prisons, and lectured worldwide. His memoir, *A Tale of Survival,* describes his far-flung and sometimes harrowing experiences.

He has authored articles about crime, psychology, sociology, sports, terrorism and travel in the *Wall Street Journal*, the *Los Angeles Examiner, the Sacramento Bee* and in scientific journals, plus ten books, including *Leisure and Popular Culture*, *Social Interaction* (C.V. Mosby), *Sexual Behavior and Family Life* (Elsevier), *Readings in Criminology* (Kendall Hunt), Humanity's Future: *The Next 25,000 Years* and, this past year, *Tried and True: The Best Travel Experiences in Europe*. He is fluent in four languages and lives in Gold River, California. His website is www.TomKando.com and he can be reached at kandotom@csus.edu.

CITY LIGHTS AND OPEN SPACES
BOB IRELAN

For me, writing a story that fit the theme of "The Americas" meant writing something about the only America I know firsthand: The United States. That's because, while I have traveled to about 20 countries, none has been in either Central or South America.

So, what to write? I got to thinking about where, over the years, I have lived and worked.

I have never lived in a large city but, before retiring, I always worked in one and liked having access to all the amenities it offered. I was energized by the heartbeat of a city. I liked the cultural and ethnic diversity cities contain. I never wanted to work in a campus or park-like setting, insulated from the cacophony of sounds and apart from crowds. Among my few regrets is that I never worked, at least for a few years, in New York City because whenever I traveled there on business, I felt a sense of urgency and electricity that seemed unique to the Big Apple.

But while I liked working in a city, I've most always lived either in a rural area or in the relative calm of suburbia. I guess that's because, as a boy growing up in Maryland, I lived in the country, bordered by a two-lane road in the front, a pair of farms on two sides, and undisturbed woodlands on the other.

Before you conclude my early years must have been marked by isolation, the fact is that rural setting was only a dozen or so miles from Washington, DC.

That set a pattern – work in the city; live outside its limits.

Over the years, this has resulted in living in Maryland for 31 years, California for 14, West Virginia for 3, back to California for 5, Texas for 9, and – since retiring in 1999,

California again. To some, this may seem like a lot of moves, but it pales in comparison to the number of moves some of my colleagues made and, for sure, to those experienced by military families.

Each of these states I lived in has its own character, beauty, and attractions. Maryland has the Chesapeake Bay, the Atlantic Ocean, Baltimore's Harbor and, yes, Maryland crab. California has the Pacific, the Sierra, Yosemite, and Lake Tahoe (where else can one snow ski in the morning and walk on an ocean beach in the late afternoon?). West Virginia has rivers full of rapids, the legendary Greenbrier resort, and the beauty of mountain after mountain. And Texas – well, it offers the Gulf, the Hill Country, the Alamo and multiple fiestas in San Antonio, and Tex-Mex cuisine.

Wherever we lived, memories formed and endured.

College meant attending the University of Maryland and living in a fraternity house for several years before crossing state lines into West Virginia to meet on a blind date the young lady who, a year later, would become my bride. Although we met in the Mountain State, she lived in Northern Virginia and both of us worked in Washington.

Our first apartment ($78.50 a month, all utilities included) was in Langley Park, Maryland, a few miles from the university and eight or so from downtown Washington. I worked in the sports department of the Washington Post, and my wife was a secretary for a lobbyist in the Nation's Capital.

Life was good. No debt. No credit cards.

The birth of our first child occurred eleven months after our marriage. That the number of months was at least nine comforted my fraternity house mother who, wanting to know which ones of "her boys" had behaved, would note on her calendar a date nine months after the date of the marriage.

Now we needed a two-bedroom apartment, which we rented in the same complex, right around the corner for $87.50. (Years later, a storage locker we rented cost the same amount.)

A second son was born three years after the first. A few months before that, we bought our first house, a three-bedroom, one bath, brick rambler in a quiet neighborhood a few miles away, in Silver Spring, Maryland. Still no credit cards, but now we had debt. To qualify for a mortgage on this $18,500 home, I needed a note from my then-employer, The Wall Street Journal, assuring I would be getting a raise to $131 a week in the next couple of months.

Several years later, believing we needed more space and fully embracing the American dream of home ownership, we sold our first home and bought a larger, nearly new one a half dozen miles away. This, we thought, would be where we would live for years and years.

Less than two years later and after a number of sleep-interrupted nights of anxiety and doubt, I bid farewell to my intended career in print journalism and accepted a corporate public relations position across the country, in Oakland, California. Once again, we opted to live beyond the big city limits, this time in a neighborhood in Walnut Creek. This was our first brand-new house – one story, four bedrooms, two-and-a-half baths, double-car garage. All this for ONLY $36,500. We would have to watch our pennies but, hey, we were itching to climb the corporate ladder.

We stayed put, house-wise for 14 years. Then came another move accompanied by a nice promotion. This time the opportunity was in West Virginia. Transfers for us were never simple. This one was more than a little complicated by the fact our two sons would not be joining us. Although both had been born in Washington, DC, they had become "California boys" – one was 21, the other 18. They had college and parttime jobs, and while they conceded West Virginia might be nice, they united in waving us on our way.

I had two offices in West Virginia, one in the capital city of Charleston and the other at a huge aluminum plant outside the small city of Ravenswood (one traffic light; population 4,100). The one-of-a-kind house we chose was in a rural community named Murraysville. It was bigger than anything we'd had before – 3,100 square feet, and set on a large lot 150 or so yards from the Ohio River. The human population of Murraysville was dwarfed by that of the deer.

After three years, I was promoted and transferred back

to the company headquarters in Oakland. That meant selling my beautiful country home for $90,000 and buying a much smaller, attached townhouse in Moraga, California, for $210,000. Ouch!

My experience with corporate transfers/promotions is that most of the time it took at least several years after each one to become financially whole. That certainly was the case moving from West Virginia back to California.

Three years later, we fell in love with a new town house development on a manmade lake in nearby San Ramon. Okay, we thought that would be where we would live for a really long time.

Sure. Less than two years later, I was transferred to Houston. We settled a few miles outside of the city, in a golf-oriented neighborhood in Sugar Land. And for nine years we enjoyed the combination of a vibrant major city and a laid-back home environment. Cultural attractions there and lasting friendships made, more than offset the discomfort of the annual "five months of August" heat and humidity.

Then came retirement. But to where? Twenty-five years earlier we had built a vacation cabin (actually, a perfectly suitable, modest-sized house) in a densely forested area of the Sierra, in California. Wherever we had moved over the ensuing years, our cabin had been a vacation destination, a spot where the family re-united.

I offered my wife what I thought was a good idea for our retirement years: continued residency in our spacious home in Texas for six months and one day each year (in part because Texas had no state income tax) and the rest of the year at our California cabin.

"Nothing doing," came the response. "California full time."

The choice, we later agreed, was perfect. A very nice primary home in the golf-oriented rural community of Rancho Murieta, 25 miles southeast of the capital city of Sacramento. It was ideal: only an hour and forty minutes' drive from our cabin and less than three hours from our favorite city, San Francisco.

That initial difficult decision to leave journalism and join the corporate life had turned out to be a good one – one that provided a lifetime of change, opportunity, and exposure to lifestyles in the East, South and West. Now in my mid-80s and enjoying the temperate climes of California, a move to the North is not in the offing.

Following 10 years of newspaper and magazine reporting and editing, including stints at The Wall Street Journal and Nation's Business magazine in Washington, DC, Bob Irelan spent 32 years managing public relations for a Fortune 500 family of companies.

In retirement, he taught a public relations course for two years at the University of the Pacific and for five years at the University of California, Davis, Extension.

He is the author of two novels. The first, *Angel's Truth – One Teenager's Quest for Justice*, was published in 2018 and took second place in Fiction at NCPA's 25th Annual Book Awards. The second, *Justifiable – Murder in the Mountain State*, was published in September 2020.

Bob's short stories are among those included in these NCPA anthologies: *Birds of a Feather, More Birds of a Feather, Destination: The World, Volumes One and Two, All Holidays 2020* and *All Holidays Vol 2*. He lives with his cat, Bai, in Rancho Murieta, California.

ALWAYS AND FOREVER

M.L. HAMILTON

Pulling into the parking lot, Emily eased into a space in front of the diner, staring at the sign. The Knotty Pine Cafe. Grimacing, she glanced over at Jonah.

"The Knotty Pine? Are you serious?"

He nodded, tilting his head sideways to look at it more closely. "It's got style."

"Style?"

"Americana, baby!"

She laughed. "Botulism, baby," she said.

"That's *not* the spirit, Em. You promised you were up for an adventure, remember?"

She gripped the steering wheel and sighed. "Okay. Let's do this." Climbing from the Outback, she pressed her hands to her lower back and stretched. The trek from Sacramento to Bakersfield had taken four and a half hours. They'd left at five AM and her bladder told her she needed the break.

Heading for the door, she pulled it open and peered inside. The entire interior was covered in knotty pine planks and crowded with tables. At nine-thirty, nearly every table was filled. Taking in the shorts, tank tops, and flip-flops, Emily figured most of the Knotty Pine Cafe's customers were tourists, although a couple of older men sipping coffee at the counter seemed like they might be locals. They wore flannel, long-sleeved shirts, sneakers, and jeans.

Shaking her head, she walked up to the podium. A harried waitress in a pink uniform went by, wearing orthopedic shoes. "Seat yourself!" she called and motioned to a booth in the corner.

Sliding into the seat, Emily reached for a napkin from the dispenser and wiped the sticky table.

Jonah looked around the room, his eyes wide with wonder. "It's perfect."

Emily lifted her brows and gave a *sure it is* nod. Reaching for the laminated menu in the holder, she glanced over the fare. She wasn't sure there was anything here she could eat. There didn't seem to be an abundance of green being served.

"Get the chicken fried steak and eggs."

Emily made a face.

"Trust me. Come on, Em, you said you'd be up for anything. Remember, breaking out of the rut, experiencing life instead of letting it rush past you."

She braced her head on her hand and stared at the menu. "This isn't what I meant," she muttered. "Paris would have worked too."

"No, no, Paris would just be doing what you've always done. Museums and sidewalk cafes and glittering lights. No, this time you've got to get dirty. You've got to really let the world sink into your pores."

She stared at his boyish face, his mop of dark hair hanging over his brow, the mischievous twinkle in his dark eyes. He twisted his mouth to the side and gave her that silly grin of his. She felt herself soften as she stared at him.

"You're ridiculous," she said.

"What?" said the waitress, appearing beside her.

Jonah snorted in amusement and ducked his head, while Emily sat up straight. "I'm sorry. I said these prices are ridiculous."

When the waitress frowned, Emily shook her head quickly. "Ridiculously good," she amended. "I mean, look at the price for...ham."

"Is that what you want?"

Emily looked at Jonah. He nodded at the menu encouragingly. Sighing, Emily set it back in its metal holder. "No, I'll have the country fried steak and eggs."

* * *

Once they were back in the car, Emily got on Interstate

61

58 heading east. She had to admit the chicken fried steak had been good – greasy and salty. She felt satiated and she'd had enough coffee to keep her going for a while.

"So, tell me about Uncle Rusty," Jonah said, shifting in the passenger seat to face her.

She glanced over, reaching up to adjust the sun visor. "He's my mother's oldest brother. He moved to Arizona in the 80s because he was sure there was going to be a nuclear war."

"Yeah, go on," said Jonah, almost bouncing with excitement.

She laughed at his enthusiasm. No one loved a good story better than he did. "So, he bought a few acres of land just outside of Flagstaff, put a mobile home on it, and built a bunker. The last time I was there, I think I was about sixteen."

"Did you see the bunker?"

"I did. He has it stocked with canned goods and paper products. I remember he had a Ham Radio, and we used it to talk to truckers on the interstate."

"That's so awesome."

She shot a grin at him. "Is anything not awesome to you?"

"It's the variety that makes life fascinating. I mean, most people hardly have enough supplies to last until Friday. They eat takeout almost every night, but here's this guy who can pretty much sustain himself."

"That's true. I think he recently installed solar and started collecting rainwater."

"Amazing."

They fell silent as the highway spread before them, scrub brush and scant trees dotting the landscape. They began climbing through the Tehachapi's, and Emily yawned widely to make her ears pop.

As they neared Barstow, Jonah sat forward in his seat, staring out the window. He pointed to a billboard along the edge of the highway. "I want to go there."

Emily squinted at it. "Calico Ghost Town?"

"Yes, I want to go to Calico Ghost Town."

"Jonah, it's out of the way. I'm already going to get into Flagstaff after five PM."

He turned and looked at her again. "How many times have you seen a ghost town?"

"Never," she said.

"And how many times after this do you think you'll get the chance?"

"It's probably a tourist trap."

"So what? Once it was a ghost town. We can walk streets that miners and saloon girls walked."

"Saloon girls?" she said, giving him a skeptical look.

"Maybe desperados. Gunslingers. Bank robbers."

She laughed. "We've already been on the road for hours, Jonah. I don't want to drive around an unfamiliar place after dark."

He gave her a stern look. "You promised…"

"Adventure," she finished for him. "Fine."

When the turnoff came for Interstate 15, she took it.

*   *   *

In the 1880s, Calico was a booming mining town, but it was abandoned after the silver bust in the 1890s. Sometime in the 1950s, a man named Walter Knott purchased it and restored all the buildings, except five of the original ones. Currently, it was maintained and operated by the San Bernardino Regional Park System.

Emily folded the brochure and placed it in her back pocket, staring out over the main street with its ramshackle adobe and wooden buildings. A few women strolled down the street in long dresses and sunbonnets, and a man wearing leather chaps with a gun holster strapped to his belt and a silver star pinned to his chest ambled by.

Jonah's eyes grew big, and he pointed at the sheriff with his thumb. Emily couldn't help but smile at his delight. They wandered through the gift stores and Jonah talked her into buying a Calico magnet for the refrigerator. Emily wasn't sure the resin exactly screamed authentic, but she didn't quibble.

Once outside, Jonah found a shack where tourists could pan for gold and he pleaded with Emily to try it. She paid for the panning and took the rusty plate from a man with a white moustache that reached below his chin.

He tipped his cowboy hat at her and said, "Good luck to you, miss. Jes' let ole Black Jack know if you're needin' any help."

"Thank you," she said, smiling. Glancing down, she noticed he wore a pair of dusty cowboy boots and dirty jeans.

Taking up a position next to a teen girl, she eyed the sluice, glancing at the girl to see what she was doing. Water ran from the top of the sluice over a bed of silt, and the girl dunked her pan into it, swishing it around in the water. Emily mimicked her motions, but after a few minutes of swishing, she didn't notice anything but brown sludge in hers. She glanced at the girl's pan, but the teenager turned her back, hiding her treasure from Emily's prying eyes.

Emily and Jonah exchanged a smile. After a few minutes of unproductive panning, Black Jack ambled over and grabbed Emily's, shifting it through the cloudy water himself. After a few minutes, he dumped a few flakes of gold into a small vial.

"Ye howdy, lookie here," he said, holding it up to the sunlight. "That'll get you a piece of candy from the mercantile."

Emily laughed with him and took the vial. "Thank you, Black Jack," she said, shooting a triumphant look at the teenager.

The teenager rolled her eyes.

Walking away from the gold panning, Jonah pointed up the street. "There's a mystery shack, Em. Let's go there next."

"Jonah, we need to get back on the road."

He stopped in the middle of the street and faced her. "How can you pass up a mystery shack, Em? Just tell me how?"

She gave him a fond smile. Lord, she loved him. "Fine. Let's go to the mystery shack."

*   *   *

The sky blazed in pink and purple glory as Emily turned into the long driveway of her uncle's property. The Ponderosa Pines created a tunnel ending at the white boxy exterior of her uncle's mobile home. She parked the Outback and opened the driver's side door as the door on the mobile home opened and her uncle stepped out.

Rusty had always been tall and lean, but his hair had gone white and receded back into a widow's peak, and he had a bit more girth around his middle than he'd had when Emily had seen him a few Christmases ago.

He climbed down the steps and onto the gravel drive, walking toward her and catching her in a bearhug. He smelled of pine and tobacco smoke as she pressed her face to the front of his flannel shirt.

"How was the drive?" his voice rumbled under her ear.

Emily clung to him, fighting back tears as she let the tension of the hours behind the wheel ease from her shoulders. "Long, but it was an adventure. You're still smoking, I see."

He made a scoffing noise. "Just one cigarette after a meal, that's all. Hardly counts."

She laughed and smoothed his collar. "It's good to see you, Uncle Rusty."

"Right back at you, Ems," he said. "Come inside. I got dinner ready. Hope you're up for pork chops and mashed potatoes."

"It sounds amazing," she said, letting him guide her toward the stairs. She'd unpack the car later.

After dinner, Rusty helped her bring her bags into the house, then they settled in front of the television. Emily let the familiar rumble of the late-night news lull her toward sleep as she thought of the next day.

When she'd planned this adventure, Rusty had agreed to go with her to the Grand Canyon. Since it was 80 miles north of Flagstaff, they planned to leave early in the morning to get there before the bulk of the tourists. She was grateful

Rusty had agreed to go with her. Despite being a man of few words, she knew her uncle was the only one who would go along with the plan without telling her it was foolish.

Rusty might not feel comfortable around crowds of people and he certainly didn't belong in a city, but when you needed someone to just get you, there was no one else who offered that quiet strength and acceptance.

Clicking off the television, Rusty looked over at her. "You wanna talk?"

She shook her head.

"Well then, I guess I'll turn in," he said, pushing himself stiffly to his feet. "You need anything, Ems, just holler."

"Thank you, Uncle Rusty."

"I'll see you tomorrow morning then."

He headed off down the hall.

Emily watched after him, then rose and went to the front door, pulling it open. She stepped onto the porch and looked out over the land her uncle had made into a refuge away from everything.

"Let's go see the bunker," said Jonah, resting his arms on the banister beside her.

Emily smiled at him. "He didn't give me permission. I can't do that."

"Sure, you can. What's he gonna say?"

Emily breathed in the pine scented air and glanced up at the vast array of stars overhead. She didn't remember the last time she'd seen so many stars.

"God, that's gorgeous," said Jonah. "Can you believe that?"

She lowered her eyes to his profile, drinking him in, remembering the first time they'd gone camping in Yosemite. He'd insisted they sleep outside the tent for the first night, snuggled together in their sleeping bags so they could watch the stars. She'd felt so safe with him, so secure, even though it seemed like the world was too vast to shelter her.

"I love you," she said softly.

He turned and smiled at her. "Love you, Em," he said. "Always and forever."

*   *   *

Rusty drove the Outback west on US 180 toward 64 north.

He'd made them a thermos of battery acid coffee and threw together biscuits with slices of bacon folded inside. Emily figured she was going to have to go on a diet when she finally got home.

Rusty shot a few glances at her as if he wanted to say something, but when she just looked out at the landscape, he turned on a country music station and tapped out the drumbeats on her steering wheel.

Emily leaned her head on her hand and dozed. Sleeping at night had become something of a misery for her. Without fail, she woke around three AM, startled out of sleep, her heart pounding, until she remembered where she was and what was happening. Last night had been no different, but when she'd awakened in Uncle Rusty's spare room, she'd heard the singing of the coyotes in the distance. The sound was so mournful, it perfectly matched her mood.

A light touch on her arm brought her around an hour later, and she blinked in the sunlight blazing through the windshield. Rusty had pulled into a parking lot, easing the Outback up to the stone barricade that blocked the canyon from the road. A scraggly mesquite bush clung to rocks on the edge of the canyon right in front of the car.

Rusty sighed and looked over at her. "This is the spot." He shot a look around the parking lot. "No one here yet. We should hurry before we attract attention."

"I have permission," she said, tapping the glove compartment with her fingernails, "but you're right. I'd rather not have to explain myself." Still, she sat, staring at the mesquite bush.

Rusty sat next to her, looking out as well. "Why here, Ems, if I can ask?"

"We came here on our honeymoon," she said, giving him a grim smile. "Rode donkeys to the bottom of the canyon and camped along the Colorado River. The next day

67

we went rafting." She laughed softly. "I thought we were going to die on the rapids, but Jonah just laughed like a lunatic."

Rusty nodded. "Sure did like adventure."

"Yeah," she said, nodding. "Sure did." She watched a red-tailed hawk floating on an updraft over the lip of the canyon. "We should do this right now." But she couldn't make her hand reach for the latch.

"Or we can sit for a while. I ain't got nowhere to be."

She curled her fingers over his forearm. "Thank you for coming with me."

He just gave her a grim smile and nodded.

Emily closed her eyes for a moment, breathing deeply, then she reached for the door handle, pushing the door open. Forcing herself to get out in a rush, she stretched, breathing in the smell of mesquite and pines, walking slowly toward the rock barricade.

Her first glimpse of the canyon took her breath away. Her eyes tracked over the layers of pink and brown cliffs disappearing away into the hazy early morning sunlight, as far as the eye could see. The enormity of it made her stomach clench, and she felt small and insignificant, gazing upon its majesty.

Rusty moved up beside her. She was aware of the thing he held in his arms, but she couldn't look at it just yet. She'd heard him retrieve it from the back of the SUV.

A breeze blew the hair back from her face, feathering across her scalp like a whisper. Twisting the wedding band around and around her ring finger, she drank in the sight, breathed in the smells, allowing the sun to warm the chill that raced through her bones.

Finally, she turned to Rusty and reached for the urn. He handed it over, his fingers briefly touching hers.

He nodded toward the Outback. "I'll just wait over there."

"Thank you," she said, her voice catching on the last word.

He patted her shoulder and walked toward the vehicle.

Emily moved to the edge of the barricade and rested

the urn on the top. It was heavier than she'd expected, and yet there was something terrible about the size of it. An entire life – dreams, hopes, plans – contained in an easy-to-carry ceramic vessel. *How conveniently and economically could someone be disposed of,* she thought bitterly.

"It's so beautiful," Jonah said, standing beside her and looking out over the canyon. "So unspeakably lovely."

She drew a shivery breath and exhaled it in a long, trembling sigh. "I don't want to do this," she said.

He turned to face her. "Em, this is the easy part. You've already survived the worst. This is..." His voice trailed off, and she looked at him.

"Is what?" she said, her eyes burning.

"Freedom." His face lifted to watch the hawk riding the thermals overhead. "Such freedom." He grinned at her, that boyish, lop-sided grin. "Earth to earth, ashes to ashes, dust to dust."

She shook her head, a tear racing down her cheek.

He moved so that he filled her entire field of view. "Em, you can do this. Let me go. You promised me. You promised me..." His voice trailed away significantly, and he gave her an encouraging nod.

"...adventure," she sobbed.

"Adventure," he repeated, reaching out to cover her hands as she opened the urn.

M.L. Hamilton teaches high school English in Central California. Since her earliest memory, books have been an integral part of her life, so pursuing a career teaching what she loved came naturally. However, she always dreamed of publishing her own novel.

That dream came true. Her first novel, *Emerald*, was published by Wild Wolf Publishing in 2010. In 2013, the Peyton Brooks' Mysteries were born, allowing her to branch into a new genre.

In addition to teaching and writing, she has three sons, two dogs, and two cats. And sometimes a stray rabbit living under her deck. If you'd like more information about ML Hamilton, visit her website at authormlhamilton.net.

WE WALK THEIR LAND

DENISE LEE BRANCO

California drew gold-seekers by the hundreds of thousands during the Gold Rush between 1848 and 1855. Many hopefuls settled in towns along the lower Merced River. One of those former towns was Merced Falls, named after the Merced River rapids, a booming community well into the 1920s, for tourists travelling into Yosemite Valley via the railroad.

Merced Falls flourished during the 1890s as a power source for several watermills located in the town. The Yosemite and Sugar Pine Lumber Company shipped lumber down from the Sierra Nevada mountains on the Yosemite Valley Railroad to two sawmills in Merced Falls, but with the construction of the Central Pacific Railroad, the town fell into disrepair like other towns that were not located by the railroad.

The Merced River rapids were beset by the building of McSwain Dam across the Merced River in 1967 to serve as a regulating reservoir for releases from Lake McClure six miles upstream, also built in 1967. Lake McSwain originated from that endeavor and resulted in a recreational community with a marina, general store, and campground, and a source for fishing and boating on the Merced River. The community of Merced Falls is nearly deserted today after McSwain Dam hindered the rapids.

My first trip to that area of rolling hills and stately oaks, and mining and milling towns of yesteryear along the Merced River occurred when I was in the first grade. A realtor invited my parents and me on a tour of cattle property, which was for sale above Lake McSwain. The concrete walls of the McSwain Dam still looked brand-new after just two years.

We hopped into the realtor's extended-cab, four-wheel drive truck and began our excursion. White rocks glittering with tiny specks of gold, and cracked with a threadlike rust color, cascaded down several hillsides, remnants of past gold mining. Jagged granite rocks rose within lush native grasses.

My most vivid memory from that trip was when we were about to leave. The realtor must have been in full-on sales pitch mode because he took his eyes off the terrain. I remember how we were all so happy sharing the magnificent characteristics of the land when the truck suddenly halted and lowered, as one of those gorgeous jagged granite rocks pierced the truck's tire like a straight pin to a balloon. There we were—way, way, way off the beaten path—involuntarily thrust into tire repair. Nevertheless, the mishap did not deter my parents. They fell in love with the beauty of the land and were at the negotiating table soon after we returned home.

The deal required that my folks build a one-mile long, four-row barbed-wire fence. I can still see my mom scooting on her bottom down steep inclines with steel fence pickets on her lap. My dad and uncle followed behind with rolls of barbed wire and a picket driver. I was a kid, so while Mom, Dad, and Uncle Tim worked, I had free rein to explore the property by horseback.

My family has a treasure trove of fond memories from spending time on our Lake McSwain property, but we all agree that the best part was never knowing which wildlife we'd be blessed to see with each visit.

I remember our first encounter with a deer herd. Few people had frequented the land for years; only cattle walked the lower parts of the acreage where feed and water were plentiful. There was no need for the deer to venture to higher ground.

We were bunched together, donned in thick winter coats in our family's blue 1968 Dodge pickup as we crossed through the property that was filled with tall native grasses that disguised the dirt road underfoot, when just over a rolling hill, my father braked. There before us were at least twenty does, fawns, and bucks grazing the hillside. We watched as each lifted their head to see what had just interrupted their serenity. Those brown beauties, in fear of the steel predator before them, pranced one by one, tails raised high, across the land and over the neighboring property's rusted barbed wire fence with the utmost grace. That will probably go down as one of the most breathtaking experiences of my life.

On one other memorable deer encounter, my bay Quarter Horse, Bill, and I were strolling along over the rolling hills when he stopped abruptly at the top of a ridge, hooves planted firmly in the ground. Imagine a horse replica in a wax museum—head held high, ears forward, eyes locked on what was directly in front of him. That was Bill. Stiff as a board. I could not get him to budge. A stare-off between prey animals ensued, but Bill won in the end as all eight deer pranced away.

Access to the Lake McSwain property required traveling through a neighboring ranch. It was a gravel road up a steep winding grade. So steep, the weight of the horse and trailer was too much for the 1968 Dodge to pull up the hill, much less hold back on descent. This may seem like an obstacle for some, but for me as a young equestrian, it was a chance to ride even more!

My father would pull the horse trailer up the gravel road a short distance, back it into a cove before unhooking the rig, and secure its wheels with granite rocks so the trailer wouldn't roll down the hill. I'd saddle up and ride behind while my folks drove to the property with hay aboard to coax our beef cattle to come in for their well-check.

Bill and I had the great fortune to save some steps and take a shortcut up a dirt cattle trail and scale lower hills to reach the gate to our property. If the trek became over-exerting for him, we'd stop for a break. I'd loosen his reins and he'd bow his head to graze. Looking back, one wonders whether Bill was truly tired and in need of a rest break or if he was a stellar actor, stopping solely because he loved eating native foothill grasses rather than his pastureland back home.

I looked forward to seeing orange California poppies reemerge every year, scattered throughout the property, in between rocks or sprouted from ground not traveled (or eaten) by cattle. I remember once stopping for our rest break near a grouping of poppies in full bloom. While my horse grazed, I picked poppies and methodically attached a bouquet of orange joy to his bridle and mane.

When I caught up to my parents inside our property, they looked at me and my decorated steed and Dad said, "It's illegal to pick poppies." Fear of arrest overcame my poppy-picking, pre-teen brain. My parents couldn't hold it together. They laughed and reassured me that I wouldn't be hauled off to the slammer. Besides, I knew we were so far off the beaten path, it would take hours for the paddy wagon to arrive. By then, the poppies would have dried, crumbled to their demise, and all evidence would disappear.

One early summer day, my trusted equine and I were strolling along a section of the property on a dirt cattle trail carved into the side of a hill. A black fuzzy California Tarantula was approaching us on the same trail. Although my father had warned me to watch for those specific tarantulas, he said they were nonpoisonous to humans. I don't care; a spider is a spider and I do not like spiders, especially big ones!

Bill's head turned towards the tarantula with eyes locked on our fellow trail hiker. Bill stepped off trail to the right ascending into the grassy hillside, never taking his eyes off the eight-legged creature until it was at least 10 feet behind us.

My family and I dreaded the dry, hot California summer months which required us to walk looking down at the ground before each step forward and even to the side. Snakes came out of hibernation after spring, with the worst period April to October each year, and though we could live with lizards darting about, rattlesnakes weren't welcomed. When we first arrived as owners of the property, we constantly walked looking at our feet, expecting to see a rattler.

I remember once walking in the tall drying post-winter

grass and coming up on a rattlesnake. The reptile was slithering along, minding its own business. I screamed and bolted in one direction; it in the other. It's funny to think that the rattler was just as afraid from my screams as I was of it.

My mom had far more run-ins with rattlesnakes than the rest of us. Once, she laid a hay flake on the ground, only to return within a few minutes to find a rattlesnake hiding underneath. Another time, she witnessed a squirrel frozen in fear while it watched a rattler trying to squeeze itself into the squirrel's dirt den. Yet another time, as Mom approached a water trough, a rattler was coiled nearby and ready to strike. She stepped back ever so slowly, narrowly avoiding becoming a snakebite victim statistic.

One year, a dirt bed about three feet in diameter mysteriously appeared in the back corner of our property, in close vicinity to a small stream. We never encountered the excavator in person but later learned through a neighbor that wild boar had been spotted on his ranch and they were the kind of animals who dug up dirt like that to stay cool.

I found myself always rotating my gaze up, around, and beneath me, being fully aware of my surroundings every time Bill and I stepped foot on the property. I knew my loyal equine's instincts would protect us, but in the back country, teamwork is critical and another set of eyes and ears always comes in handy.

I can still see in my mind's eye one solitary bobcat trotting across the top of the highest hill on the property while I was leisurely riding Bill on the winding dirt road of an adjacent hill. I'd rather not see a bobcat face-to-face but after first witnessing one, I loved analyzing dirt on the property for paw marks. Bobcats have claws that retract, so their impression would be that of four toes. I transformed into my favorite sleuth, Nancy Drew, and stayed on the lookout for bobcat tracks.

I thank my parents for a childhood filled with incredible experiences in nature; not every kid gets to say that. I am grateful for the honor of witnessing God's beautiful creatures living their best life, wild and free. Although the property above Lake McSwain was purchased by my family for our cattle, and though the California Gold Rush settlers blasted hillsides in search of gold riches, the land never really belonged to any of us. We were just visitors in wildlife habitat, given the privilege to enter.

My prayer is that all future generations continue to respect the wildlife that live among the oaks and roam free in the rolling hills above Lake McSwain. It is and always will be their land; we are merely their guests.

Denise Lee Branco is an award-winning author and inspirational speaker, who continues to believe, dream, and overcome so those who meet her recognize the possibilities within them. Denise's first book, Horse at the Corner Post: Our Divine Journey, won a silver medal in the Living Now Book Awards.

Denise is a longtime member of Northern California Publishers and Authors and a current member of several other writing and publishing organizations. She has been a contributor to multiple anthologies.

Denise is currently working on her next book, The Ride to Purpose: Finding Freedom on the Trail of Life. She lives in the foothills of Northern California and loves biking on nature trails, foods with melted cheese, and spoiling her three rescues.

Visit www.DeniseInspiresYou.com to learn more.

CALIFORNIA GIRLS
DANITA MOON

L iving in California since I was two years old, I was accustomed to all the brown grass and trees that weren't very green.

When I flew to North Carolina for my grandparents' 50th wedding anniversary it was a bit of a shock to see so much green.

It was my first time on an airplane, so the trip was full of firsts.

My sister and I stayed for a month since we had never met our dad's parents or anyone else on his side of the family.

The pace in North Carolina is slower than in California. The small town of Snow Camp where my grandparents lived was an exceedingly small community and we met all our relatives.

It was as if we stepped back in time. My great-aunt Sarah made homemade ice cream that was to die for. My grandmother belonged to a quilting circle, who hand quilted rather than use a sewing machine. That is when I learned how to quilt, but I haven't done any quilting since my grandmother passed away.

This trip is when I first learned about the Quaker religion also known as The Friends of the Church. After going to church services here in California, the ones in North Carolina were far different.

My grandmother was a very proper woman, so we always called them Grandmother and Grandfather. She also hated telling people the name of the street they lived on because it was Old Dam Road. I always found this hilarious.

They lived on acres, so we were miles away from any neighbors, and I shot my first and only gun behind their home. My grandfather showed us how to hold and shoot a gun properly. Not only did I learn to shoot, but I also drove a tractor for the first time, and it was so much fun. I wasn't even driving a car yet.

This one-month trip was a gift for my high school graduation and was a bit overwhelming to meet so much family at once: great-aunts and uncles, aunts and uncles, as well as all my cousins.

There was so much food I had never tried before: fried okra, clams, homemade pimento cheese, barbeque pork sandwiches with coleslaw on top, and so much more. I still can vividly see The Kitchen, the restaurant that we went to frequently.

Besides Snow Camp we visited Graham, Winston Salem, Raleigh, Durham, Greensboro, and other parts of the state.

The weather in July is extremely hot, but the humidity in North Carolina makes it feel even hotter. I would not be able to manage it today as I did when I was eighteen.

My grandparents 50th wedding anniversary party was a true family reunion – the first time they had all but one of their grandchildren gathered. My brother was in the Army and stationed in Germany. When we had a photo done it was my grandparents, their children (my dad, his brothers and sister) and seven of their eight grandchildren.

North Carolina has a huge celebration for the 4th of July which includes a big parade. My sister and I rode in the parade sitting on the back of my Uncle Cletus's red convertible with a sign that said "California Girls."

Not only was the parade such a big gathering but they also had an outdoor theater. The play was *Sword of Peace* and the theater reminded me of colosseums that you see on television. There were stone seats that appeared to be steps.

Being a huge fan of *Little House on the Prairie*, I felt as though I had stepped back into the 1800s when I arrived at my grandparents' place and was amazed at the forest of trees that encompassed their house. It was red brick, with the front and back porch built out of solid wood, which led to the most amazing view of mother nature when you stepped out the door. It was great to see that my grandfather had hunting dogs as well as puppies. The whole bunch of them greeted us when we went out to see the back of their property.

My mom and brother lived with my grandparents while my dad was in Vietnam and my brother was just a toddler. I wouldn't arrive for another couple of years, but I remember my mom telling stories of when she lived there.

The one thing that stands out is that when there was a thunder and lightning storm do not wash your hair or anything in the sink as lightning can pass through the water and the pipes. How could this be I thought, but lo and behold during our visit, was a thunderstorm, complete with lightning and sure enough, it came through the light sockets and everything. I was a bit surprised when it happened.

Growing up as the middle child with two siblings with dark hair and me with strawberry blonde hair and blue eyes, it was always in the back of my mind that I might be the red-headed stepchild. This made sense at the time as my parents were divorced. My grandmother solved the mystery while looking at pictures during our month-long visit and she showed me a picture of her at 18, which was how old I was then, and we could have been twins. From that point on I never had that nagging thought again.

Making this trip was a godsend as my grandfather passed away shortly after their 53rd wedding anniversary, and that had been the first and only time I would see him. My grandmother and I were always close. Our birthdays were just a day and fifty years apart. I look back at photos of additional trips that I made to see her after my grandfather passed and when she came to California, which reminds me of how much I was like her. We celebrated our birthdays together both in North Carolina and in California. On one of these birthdays, she gave me her wedding ring that she wore for over fifty years. I have never married, but I have it to pass down to another generation of our family.

My grandmother not only lost her husband of over fifty years, but she also lost her son, my father, when he was 49 years old. It took a toll on her, and I wouldn't see her in California again after his death, but I did visit her again. My last visit to North Carolina was just before 9/11. I was there for a couple of days after this tragic event that shook America to its core, and we comforted each other as we all tried to come to grips with what had happened, and to watch as the number of lives lost that tragic day rose. I flew home days after 9/11 and this would be the last time I would see my grandmother in person. She passed away before I could make another trip out there.

I would like to think I left a bit of California with my family during this month-long visit from memories that I had shared. I know I brought back North Carolina memories. I will always remember riding in that red convertible with the "California Girls" sign hanging off the side.

Danita Moon is a certified proofreader and is a virtual assistant. She had her first story, Sent by an Angel, published in NCPA's *More Birds of a Feather* anthology.

She is currently working on her first book, *Through the Looking Glass*, which follows her journey from being diagnosed with a mental illness and her goal of helping to stop the stigma associated with it. Her goal is to have it published by 2023. Danita also volunteers in the California Author Booth every year at the California State Fair. She is a true booklover.

FINDING MY ITALIAN NATURE
IN BRAZIL

LINDA VILLATORE

My aunt Aurora said, "You always have your head in the clouds."

It's true.

At six, I was taken to the Hayden Planetarium in New York City and touched the black meteorite at its entrance. The rock had dangerously fallen from space, yet was not considered a sacred object. I touched it and felt the stars. I've always struggled to keep my feet on the ground.

From that meteoric, in every sense, moment, I have been aware of living on a planet floating around in the blackness of space. Traveling throughout the world, observing cultures, I learned that no matter where they are, people share most things in life. They want to live in peace, hope for a better life for their children. They believe in a god who watches over them and differ only in whose god is real.

Tucked deep into a lush valley south of Rome, the mountain town of Popoli was the site of three rivers. There was so much water that pipes jammed into the rocks made fountains which flowed all year long. Throughout history, Popoli was a strategic pinch point blocking entry to Rome from the south. It therefore suffered convulsive fighting by Nazis trying to hold back the Allied armies who were grinding and bombing their way north. When I visited there in the 1970s, my uncles were still angry with the Germans.

For two thousand years of settlement, there was no Italy at all. The peninsula churned with warring medieval cities, conquests by Austria, France, the Moors, the Popes, and the Greeks until Italy was united into a fragile confederation in the 1850s. During the chaotic years that followed, shifting power struggles made life hard for most people, including my relatives. So, by the great diaspora of the early 1900s, my restless grandfather, tired of sleeping on the floor, took his bride and three-year-old daughter out of Popoli. They boarded a ship to New York City, not Rio de Janeiro.

Strangely, this choice shaped the potential within my personality and changed the expression of my genes. The following story is how I came to learn that.

* * *

It was a misty morning in the Pacific rainforest of northern California where I now lived. The fog proudly lifted to reveal its gift of a clear blue sky. The pure air was not ruffled by the slightest breeze and the song of the Swainson's thrush echoed through the canyon below.

I turned on my computer and found an email from Brazil, from a Karin Villatore.

The woman writing had the same last name as mine and was politely inquiring if we might be related. She thought I might be a famous singer. She'd found my name on a musician's website. I did sing, but was not famous. At first suspicious of her motives, I was won over by her English grammar and courtesy in her second email.

As Dante noted about the soul's journey to heaven, politeness is found in greater abundance as you get closer to heaven.

Turns out we had things in common. She was a third-generation Italian immigrant. She had been to the US. She had her own business, an advertising agency, also like me.

"Tell me about your life," she wrote. So, against my usual shyness and desire for privacy, I responded in some detail. Within a minute, she replied. "I want to meet you in person!" She would come north in a few weeks.

And so, she did for one month. We spent happy, casual days together around northern California. In Yosemite, she was distinctly unimpressed with Rainbow Falls. I later found out that the Falls of Iguacu (AKA Iguazu) roar all year long.

The highlight of her trip was seeing a bear run across the road.

There are no bears in South America.

A year later, at Christmastime, I went to Brazil to visit Karin. Although we never found out if we were truly related, we had agreed that we could be cousins.

South America isn't directly south of us, as you might think. It's offset to the east into the Atlantic Ocean.

* * *

Continents are light and float on tectonic plates. Astride its tectonic plate, Brazil cracked off Africa on a ride millions of years ago and was pushed across the Atlantic by the zipper-like volcanic seam erupting under the Atlantic, the mid-oceanic ridge. You'll find that seam today. It runs along the west coast of Africa and exactly matches up with the east coast of Brazil. Along that seam where the plants and soil match up) is the evidence of that rupture a long time ago, when Brazil left Africa.

* * *

It was an arduous night-flight south and across the full bosom of Brazil. In the blackness, angry thunderheads rose from the jungle below. Surrounding our plane, they pushed and shoved each other. They growled, and threatened. They flashed each other with lightening. Understandably, the god Thor was feared in his day. All the roaring and flashing kept me awake, with my little nose pressed against the cabin window as our pilot was weaving through them.

I arrived in Curitiba, Brazil late afternoon after a 14-hour flight.

My lanky cousin, Karin, was easy to spot in the terminal. A world traveler, she quickly handled my baggage and whisked me off into town in her small car.

My body still buzzing from the flight, we sat down at a small café on a tree-lined street. She ordered *Caipirinhas*. This refreshing national drink is made with mashed limes, skin and all, cachaça (a fermented sugar cane liquor), sugar, and crushed ice.

It's truth serum.

"Tell me everything!" We sat in the slanting afternoon sun while she hungrily asked catch-up questions. The first Caipirinha went down quickly, the flight already forgotten. She ordered again. As I sipped the second, I felt exuberant and happy. I saw myself seated at a sunny table in Brazil with a friend. It was a good day.

Karin lives in the temperate climate zone of Brazil, south of Rio. Curitiba is an upscale university city, known for its environmental consciousness. School children hold hands as they walk to school. Old people walk arm in arm. When they meet, people kiss on the street in greeting.

She also taught media relations at the university, and every Friday after work Karin and her colleagues unwound with drinks and laughter at their favorite café. They had been doing this for years. It's more of a Latin culture in Brazil, more demonstrably affectionate than in the north.

As a North American of Italian descent, I am cooler, more rational…less warm than the Italians who populate Brazil. The puritanical influences at the heart of North America are more aggressive, less affectionate than the lusty, freewheeling Latin society of Brazil.

She was a single mother. I was not. She shared a two-bedroom apartment with her eleven-year-old mixed race son Gabriel in a new building with numbered underground parking for residents. She had the same appliances, which were slightly smaller than ours here. Half of the city was still being built. A few high-rise office buildings mushroomed in the skyline miles away.

There were many healthy living trees in Curitiba. Judging by their uniform height and shape, they looked like they'd all been planted together about 15 years ago. Curitiba had a new sports stadium for ever-popular soccer matches. Karin took me to a soccer match. I was impressed with the well-groomed and well-mannered fans. She also took me to a concert at a fine new concert hall. We had to sit through a boring politician speak for an hour before we were permitted to see the concert. This was a common practice, I was told. Americans would never put up with it.

Curitiba has a world-class museum designed by Oscar Niemeyer. In that museum, I found two haunting objects which seemed to hint at the country's historical sensibility. One artifact was a metal helmet, the type worn by the Portuguese conquistadors who ravaged the country 600 years ago. Sitting there without two human eyes inside directing it, the thing was frightening.

The other object was a statue of a woman's pelvis. It was cut off and showed no waist or the knees, just the uterus on one side, the hips, and the buttocks cheeks around back. The buttocks cheeks were high and rounded. It is the African shape. It evolved in Africa to store and provide nourishment to the human being during times of extreme starvation and famine. This shape is so highly prized in Brazil, and now around the world as erotica, that women endure dangerous implants of fat and silicone to achieve it.

New construction in Curitiba was everywhere. Tall cranes waved in the air. All the pleasant single-story houses on the streets near Karin's apartment were protected by metal gates and fences. Clearly there was a class divide more extreme than here in the U.S. On this same street one morning I saw two deeply black laborers lifting cut paving stones from a pile of such stones stacked along the curb. They set down each stone in its place on a leveled sandy base. The result would be a new, but old style, stone paved sidewalk. Of course, this paving method takes longer, but such stonework is beautiful. It lets the rainwater flow through. It reduces flooding and erosion, and nurtures the trees. They were not pouring concrete as we would have done in the U.S. These black men were doing hard labor on the street with gated fences. The segregation between races in Brazil is evident, yet sometimes nuanced in a mix with the indigenous tribes. It's clearly different than in the history of northern slavery, though Brazilians put their native people on reservations like we do.

Across the street from Karin's modern building was a cemetery. I strolled through its lumpy grounds one morning.

The tilted headstones and worn mausoleums with Portuguese names spoke of an old Brazil with its roots firmly in a colonial past.

In fact, Brazil is a creative, thrusting country. But it is saddled with the archaic Portuguese language. How many people in the world want to learn Portuguese? In order to do business or be considered educated, one must speak English.

I learned Portuguese enough to sing in it. I sing the beautiful bossa nova melodies of Antonio Carlos Jobim, a Brazilian gift to the world; bossa nova is a soft swaying motion of tender romance. That is how my cousin first found me.

Twenty miles inland from the Atlantic coast, Curitiba has only a few native trees left of the once vast Atlantic rain forest. The dense conifer forest once ran south and north along the east coast for hundreds of miles. It was found north, past Rio, until it dried out when it reached the heat of the tropics. I was curious to see the remains of that forest, so Karin arranged for a friend to drive me to a preserve.

Knowing Brazil's poor history of conservation, I was prepared for disappointment at this patch of former glory. Brazil's poor record of corruption and environmental degradation began over 500 years earlier with the Portuguese conquerors. And like our own history, a force with superior weaponry, dedicated to itself, overran the indigenous people, enslaving them, mating with them, and taking their land. The short and incredibly sweet native people of Brazil who remain live on reservations.

On another night, over more sips of the universal truth serum, Karin confided.

"You are lucky in the United States that you were colonized by the British and not the Portuguese."

"Why?"

Karin elaborated. "The British hold some respect for nature. They share the idea of having public parks. They left roads and bridges, and introduced their system of fairness under the law."

According to Karin, this taste of fairness and

democracy was never part of the mix in Brazil. The Portuguese were cruel beyond belief. They gutted the country. They took everything and left great swaths of wasteland. One large state in the center of the country is named *Minas Gerais;* it means General Mines.

I came to realize that the U.S. is fortunate in two other respects as well: America's natural geography and location on our planet. Our mountain ranges run north to south, which permits transit through their low passes. While almost of equal size, America spreads squarely across the temperate zone. This gives us a favorable agricultural climate and a mostly comfortable one to live in. Most of Brazil's land mass lies in the oppressive equatorial heat, and there are no mountain ranges at all.

All was not as it appeared however. Below the equator ("the line" they call it), there is envy of the US...bitterness mixed with their national pride. They feel left behind. At the same time, countries below the equator brag that there are no nuclear weapons below the equator. The "line" is part of their lore in popular songs and writing.

Traveling with an open heart and mind was a chance to learn about differences, my history, and how one thing affects another. I had a chance to learn about the choices my Italian grandparents made.

 Award-winning educator with over 30 years of experience in custom web based and classroom instructional design and training, Linda is an author of several acclaimed activity-based courses, has been published in multi-media, staffing and production magazines. She is also an award-winning dramatic actress and stage director, as well as a documentary television producer with high-level expertise in communication and media production. She now specializes in executive coaching, strategic planning, facilitation, and project management.

Linda has taught in universities, community colleges, and the public and private sector for clients in over 40 industries. Awarded by the U. S. Army for educational counseling, she was nominated for the California *Governor's Award for Environmental Economic Leadership, Who's Who* in *American Colleges and Universities,* and played competition chess with Bobbie Fischer at the age of seven.

DESTINED TO ALWAYS BE A "LATENIK"

NORMA JEAN THORNTON

With the exception of one year, for the first five years after my divorce, the first weekend after school was out, my two young kids would fly alone from Sacramento to San Bernardino to spend their entire summer vacations being spoiled by my middle-sister and brother-in-law. That not only gave the kids quality time with their childless aunt and uncle, but also a yearly endless period of fun and games for all at Disneyland and the La Brea Tar Pits, the great Farmers Markets, trips to Tijuana, the ocean, Norton AFB to see the planes where their uncle was stationed, and anywhere and anything else the four of them could think of.

Including riding their uncle's motorcycle, and one year, even a trip to the ER to set a broken arm for my son because of something to do with a tree he and his uncle were playing in … or with.

For me, in order to keep a roof over our heads, it was a time to work my fool head off each year at the two consecutive full-time jobs with Levitz Furniture Store, and later, Weinstocks Department Store, plus the numerous seasonal and part-time jobs I had through the Theatrical Employees B-66 Union that enveloped cashiers, which I was one of, and included both the Sacramento County Fair and the CA State Fair, the Sacramento Solons Baseball Team, West Capitol Speedway, the Sacramento Capitols Semi-Pro Football team and the Starlite Drive-in Theatre. I was also a cocktail waitress at the Hawaiian Hut in West Sacramento, a food waitress at the Carl Greer Inn in Sacramento and a sandwich maker at Tony Baloney's in

North Sacramento, plus a few more miscellaneous part-time jobs.

For variety, the third year we decided to let the kids go by train to San Bernardino, but for some reason, Sacramento didn't have a train station, or if it did, it at least had no train leaving for San Bernardino in the late spring of 1973, so we had to go to Stockton to their train station. My then-fiancé's family lived in Ceres, so we were going to make a day of it, and after putting my two on the train, we would take his four kids on down to Ceres to visit his family.

Then-fiancé, and later-hubby, Wayne, always felt that unless one was at least fifteen minutes early to get to wherever one was going, one was late. My theory has always been, as long as I'm slipping in the door one minute to within ten minutes after the dedicated/ suggested time to be there, we were all lucky!

Going on his theory, we left very early that morning to get to the train station a full hour ahead of the scheduled arrival time to purchase tickets and board the train to San Bernardino. Once there, out of character by having free time, I leisurely sauntered to the ticket counter, which had a line of all those early arrivers, who would NOT have been there had we gotten there late.

Two tickets procured and tucked away safely in the little envelope that went with them, instead of my normal rushed pace, I had time to slowly meander back to the car, where six bored, anxious kids and one very-pleased-because-we-got-there-early-fiancé were waiting for me.

Showing them the tickets, then putting them back in the envelope, I stood outside the driver's side, window down, leaning in talking, with the envelope-filled-with-tickets in my hand, for a full thirty minutes before the train pulled in.

Something I wouldn't have had time for, had we gotten there at my prescribed time – not an hour early, that's for sure!

While taking the kids to get them settled on the train, I opened the envelope to get the tickets … and … NO TICKETS! What happened to them and where had they gone?! That envelope had not been out of my hands!

We rushed back to the car, looking on the ground the entire way, to no avail, yelling for Wayne and the other four kids to help look for the tickets! After rethinking the entire scenario, I remembered that I had been tapping the envelope where I was resting my arms as I leaned against the car, and the only conclusion was those tickets must have slipped out of the envelope and dropped down inside the driver's side door.

Fortunately, Wayne had tools and could take the door apart to get to those tickets, that most certainly, were right down inside the door, along with the rolled-down window. I grabbed the tickets and the kids' hands, and literally had to run to catch the train, which had already blown its warning whistle.

By that time, the train was pretty-much filled with existing passengers, plus those loading in Stockton, and the car we got on only had one seat available. It was a fairly large seat, and my two were fairly small kids, so rather than take a chance on not getting a seat in another car, I told them to stay put, and I'd go look for two seats in the car ahead. Leaving my purse with the kids, I started to get off the train, then decided that probably wasn't a wise idea in case somebody tried to snatch it from two little kids, so I ran back and grabbed it, then hopped off that car and ran to the one ahead.

Just as I got aboard, the train jerked and started moving, with me inside! I was yelling, *"STOP! I NEED TO GET OFF! MY KIDS ARE IN ANOTHER CAR!"* ... all to no avail. It just kept picking up steam! However, a conductor outside saw my plight, or most likely heard my screeches, and ran alongside the train, yelled for me to take his hand, and he basically pulled me off the train just before it picked up too much speed to safely do what we were about to do! The guy was going at a full-run, and I almost fell jumping off the damned thing.

The worst thing, though, was I looked up, just as the car my kids were in sped by, with four small hands and two little noses pressed up against the window and a shocked, terrified look on their poor little, barely 10- and 11-year-old faces. I'm not a crier, but I burst into tears as images of all the horrible things that could happen to them quickly scrolled through my mind – foremost, that I didn't even get to tell them goodbye, I loved them, nor give them ANY instructions on what to do, or what not to do. At that time there were no cell phones, or they definitely would have had one with them!

I was miserable and on pins and needles the rest of the day, and until later that night when my sis finally called to tell me they had made it safely – and then, to make matters even worse than they already were, I was shocked again when she reamed me out, asking "Why in the Hell did you let those kids go alone on a Greyhound bus?!"

WHAT?

Nothing at all was mentioned by Amtrak that the train would deboard in Bakersfield, where the train would continue on in a different direction, but anyone going down to the area where my kids were, had to finish that leg of the trip by bus.

Another of those you don't know what you don't know, and I definitely didn't know to ask them if the train went all the way to the large town of San Bernardino, with two young unaccompanied children aboard! One would think that would just be a given. Either that, or they should have told me when I first called to enquire about two kids traveling alone on Amtrak, to San Bernardino. Plus, it isn't as though we didn't have the time for them to bring up that conversation when I actually purchased the tickets for two young children, ages given, traveling alone.

And the takeaway from all of that? It never fails – I'm always late! Had we not gotten there early, I wouldn't have had time to tap the tickets and lose them inside the car door, which made us late anyway – probably even later than I might have made us by getting there at my normal time!

An addendum:

My son, later that year when he was still 10, traveled with my youngest sis and her Air Force hubby and *their* son to Minot, North Dakota to their new airbase, and spent a week with them during Christmas vacation, before flying

94

alone back to Sacramento. I was surprised – and instantly scared – when I received a phone call from PSA airlines, asking if I had a son on their flight. They quickly advised me that everything was okay, but he had *insisted* they HAD to call his mommy, because she'd be worried. The pilot had announced onboard there had been some kind of minor delay in leaving but there would be no delay in destination arrivals, and it concerned my son, even though they explained to him that it wasn't going to affect his arrival in Sacramento.

He persisted and made them promise they'd call me. Poor little guy – that earlier train situation upsetting me was surely still on his mind, but what it did was scare me even more just to receive a phone call from the airlines, asking about my very young child. I'm forever grateful they did, though. Especially after that train fiasco!

PSA also let him visit the cockpit in-flight and talk to the pilot, and, as usual, he came home with another set of wings pinned to his shirt.

Amtrak displeased me no-end regarding their safety for kids; quite the opposite of PSA.

Her baby sister called her Nonie, her great-granddaughter calls her GumGum.

Norma Jean Thornton, AKA Noniedoodles, a multiple County and State Fair award-winning baker, candy-maker, art-doodler, plus award-winning writing granny from Rio Linda, California, creates her doodle-art and dabbles with her writings at the computer, with unwanted help from her feisty cats.

normathornton@yahoo.com   lulu.com/spotlight/nonie

*"*Love Never Dies*" in Harlequin's Inspirational Anthology, A Kiss Under the Mistletoe
Nonie's Big Bottom Girls' Rio Linda Cookbooks (4)
Nonie's "Stuff" Cookbooks (Candy &…Stuff; Cookies…&…Stuff; Soups &…Stuff)
Nosie Rosie's Diaries: (True cat diaries, written by The Granny & The Windy) (Years 1 & 2)
Nonie's Cat Anthologies (Fun, not-so-fun, sometimes crazy short cat stories) 2 Volumes
Nonie's Wet Kitty Kisses Anthologies (Mostly humorous Shorts) 2 Volumes
noniedoodles coloring books (artwork by Nonie's original doodles) Several Volumes
Doodles the Dorky Dragon, in the Dorky Land of Noniedoodles
Just What is a Critique Group? A Writer's Symbiotic Relationship! … Do I Need One, or Not?
Every 2019, 2020, 2021, 2022 & 2023 NCPA Anthology

UNFINISHED BUSINESS

ROSEMARY COVINGTON MORGAN

Central South Carolina
Present Day

"This heat will kill you, little girl. Why don't you let one of the menfolk drive you back to your hotel?"

Krista shook her head. "Thanks, Aunt Sheila. I run five miles every day. Surely, I can walk a mile." In truth, Krista was sick of the family reunion. As a historian, she thought she'd be more interested. *One more question about my parents and grandparents, another session of explaining how I'm related to this one or that one, and I'll burst, or at least say something nasty.* The machinations of getting a ride would take at least half an hour more than she could stand.

She'd never been to one of these reunions, nor had her parents. This reunion was for her mother's side of the family, and Mother hadn't been interested.

Her father's family lived in Ohio for generations, and, as far as he knew, there were no family members for a reunion.

Her parents, Susan and Carl, thought they had escaped the oppression that clouded the brains of many black people. They wanted no reminders. Krista often wondered what they were thinking when the police wrongfully burst into their home one early morning looking for drugs—killing them both.

Did her mother say in her cultured voice, "Oh, dear, you have the wrong people," before they shot her in the head? Krista couldn't imagine what her professor father said in his eloquent voice before taking six bullets to the chest while holding an empty gun. And she would never know since the police body cams all malfunctioned.

This year's family reunion was at the South Carolina plantation home of their ancestors. While Krista thought the location was a strange, uncomfortable selection, she had to admit to being taken by the beauty of the place. The surroundings embraced the heat of a southern summer – white buildings, abundant plant life, marble benches under shade trees. Combined heat and humidity produced a surreal haze that enveloped the scene. The plantation building and grounds had been someone's idea of paradise.

Enchantment surrounded her as she stood in front of the Corinthian columned mansion with a wrap-around portico designed to catch breezes. A four-tiered marble fountain carved with playful cherubs sprinkled musical springs of water into a marble bowl. A garden of red and yellow roses encircled the fountain bowl.

Closely trimmed Kentucky Bluegrass covered the slightly sloped lawn. An oak tree canopy shaded a path that once provided the approach for elegant horse-drawn carriages.

She walked beneath the tree canopy, eyeing the dormant cotton fields in the distance. Small wooden slave cabins stood to the side. Yesterday's family tour of the cabins offered no real insight into people who once lived there. Yet, her relatives were fascinated. Some took the docent up on an offer to spend the night in the cabins. To Krista, it was like sleeping in someone's grave. But, today, she wanted to take a second look at the homes of her ancestors.

Three cabins had been refurbished and opened for public viewing. There were four more standing, supposedly off-limits. Since the plantation was once home to six-hundred enslaved people, Krista assumed property owners had destroyed the other cabins.

Curious, Krista went to the door of one of the off-limit cabins and instinctively knocked. To her surprise, a whispered male voice said, "Come in." *My mind is playing tricks on me in this heat!*

She opened the door, expecting to find someone

inside. There was no one. The cabins she visited the day before were attractively rehabilitated and each looked to be for a single, small family. In at least a century, no one had touched this one. Ancient-looking nails and splinters protruded from the floorboards, wooden planks above and below the windows were missing. Mud adhesive, sparsely visible between the siding planks, allowed a clear view of the yard in front of the building.

Krista was shocked by how familiar she found the place. Sensing an invitation to take a seat, she lowered herself onto an unsteady, dust-covered, wooden chair. She knew the cabin once provided a home for many inhabitants. The energy of invisible people once living in the home embraced her.

Peering through the crumbling siding planks, she was startled by a strange yet familiar sight. Dogs, chickens, and small children busied themselves in front of her. She looked closer to see a group of people walking toward the cabins. *They have just spent a long, hot, stifling day working in the cotton fields.* There was unease and anxiety within their aura. She could also feel a distant kinship with their faith, innate strength, and compassion. But with every step, sadness lurked, calling to Krista.

Sorrow shrouded her. For the first time, the pressing weight and agony of her parent's death became overwhelming. Visualizing their death as never before, she experienced the suddenness, felt the pain and anguish as each reached for the other, sinking to the floor together in death, praying to a higher power.

Inside the dream-like trance, Krista was screaming. What was happening? Why this dream? Why now? She snapped back to the present, trembling, confused. *I'm not accustomed to this kind of heat and humidity. That's all this is. I probably need a nap.*

To put some distance between herself and the reunion, Krista had rented a room at a bed and breakfast near the plantation but away from her family. Fortunately, there was cold lemonade waiting when she walked through the door.

Her body was weak after the cabin experience. The

walk back to the B&B was vague.

Krista felt she was being followed. The cold lemonade relaxed her, and she was beginning to feel normal. A cooling breeze and stunning golden sunset encouraged her to take the lemonade to the porch and sit on its swing. Before long, she was dozing.

*   *   *

"I always wanted to do this," said the young man sitting on the swing with her, "So did you." The young man sounded familiar, but Krista couldn't see his face. *Is he real? No, I'm dreaming or hallucinating again.*

The man continued, "This was the overseer's cabin, but he never did much more than sleep here. This swing hung here, lonely and inviting."

Krista looked around at what had earlier been a delightful porch full of geranium and petunias surrounded by a lawn of manicured grass. What she saw now was a gray, neglected porch covered in bird poop and a house that hadn't been painted in forever—no grass in sight.

"You're tired, little sistah," the man said. "Go get some sleep; we'll talk later."

It was now night, and she sat on a bench in a grove of magnolia trees. Enjoying their pleasant scent, she noticed the young man from the swing walking toward her, smiling. *I'm having a nice dream now. After the horror of the cabin dream, I deserve a nice dream.*

"It's not a dream," the young man said. "None of it. But cheer up; this was one of our favorite places to hide."

"How so?" Krista asked, noticing her easy conversation with this person or *whatever.*

"You were a cook and I brought food from the vegetable gardens and smokehouse to the cooks." He was seated beside her now. "We saw each other every day and would plot to be together when our work was done. You always wanted us to come here."

His facial features became clearer. She knew his smooth ebony skin, brown eyes, broad nose, strong teeth, and the small mole between his eyebrows. Quame. Passion reminded her. *I know his name, it's Quame. I know him as well as myself.* She lifted a hand to touch his face. Feeling the touch of her hand on the rough stubble of his face felt wonderful, but it wasn't her hand. The hand was younger, lighter skinned, rougher, not the hand she knew as hers — chocolate-colored, manicured.

"You probably look different in your present. I can only see you as I remember," Quame said. "Much of what you see now is through my eyes. I use your modern language to voice my words so you can understand. That may seem new, but it's not. We could communicate without words."

"I need to understand this, Quame. If this isn't a dream, then I'm crazy or caught in some sort of time warp thing, which also means I'm crazy."

"Try the time warp thing," he spoke quietly, his voice soothing. "You aren't crazy. When you walked into the cabin this afternoon, you drifted into your past, and I was able to find you."

They were walking now. "So, I've warped into a fairytale and found my long-lost prince?"

"I was never a prince, far from it. I was a regular field hand with a few privileges that let me see you nearly every day. Our life was far from a fairytale unless the tale included a lot of hate, dread, and punishment.

"But we always had joy, Krista. We had each other to fight off the horrors. We bonded from when you were born, and I was two years old. And I'm sure I spent those two years waiting for you to come, just as I've spent the last two hundred years waiting for you to come. I was worried at first. You seemed so distant, so cynical, so unhappy. Connecting with the experience of your parents was critical. You needed that experience to release you from the bitterness that was keeping you from feeling and expanding your vision beyond the buried grief controlling your present."

"Beyond the possible," Krista responded quietly, matching the tone of Quame's ethereal voice, "To a time where we loved each other so completely that we became one being." She hesitated then said, "I remember."

101

The landscapers had designed the garden around paths lined with camellias, rhododendron, and roses. They walked through the lovely garden silently, words unnecessary, minds melded, seeing through each other's eyes, reading each other's thoughts.

Krista looked toward the sky and stopped. "Look at the stars, Quame. There are millions of them! SOOO bright. They're all around us! I can touch them." She began to run, reaching as if trying to catch one. "Quame, we're in a bubble surrounded by stars." Excitement coursed through her body, arousing a burst of energy. She was bouncing with giggles and glee.

He put a calming hand on her shoulder. "Time jumps around randomly in this 'time warp.' You're six years old, Krista. You have a memory from when you were six."

"When I was six?"

"We had run away from Sunday supper, and you became dazzled by the starlight. We came to watch for weeks until you found something else to fascinate you."

"Like what?"

"Butterflies, rocks, small animals, the moon. You were always excited by something."

"Like this?" Krista stood in front of Quame, reached for his neck, and brought his lips to hers.

Lips and tongues touching, arms wrapped tightly around each other, Krista's passion was moving her to weakness, sinking more into his arms. They remained entwined, pulling energy from one another until they both nearly fell.

Quame laughed. "That didn't happen until you were fifteen." Krista joined him in joyous laughter as their bodies seemed to float.

"Hopefully, it happened a lot."

"It did. We made a child."

They walked some more. "Where's the fountain?" Krista asked.

Quame hesitantly said, "It wasn't here during this time."

Krista looked to find the mansion house bright with light, violins, and a piano playing.

"How old are we now?" she asked.

"You are about sixteen, and I am eighteen."

"Let's dance," she said. She tried to snuggle but found she couldn't.

"You're having our baby," blushing, he said, "Let's try dancing anyway."

They danced awkwardly, trying to move in unison across the grass with the baby pressed between them. They stumbled, and the baby kicked. They both felt it and began laughing, falling onto the grass, into the moon's brightness.

"This was our last night." His mood changed; the moon's brightness became clouds. Quame barely uttered, "We don't know yet, but tomorrow, me and two other hands get sold. They needed the money to pay for the fountain you like so much."

They were again seated on the swing at the overseer's house. "What happens to us?" Krista pleaded.

"There is no more us. I don't have memories beyond that night."

"So, what does that mean?"

"You would have awakened to find me gone. We had no goodbye. I would remember. I was probably sent off early morning to avoid trouble with family, friends. There would have been anger. I don't know what happened after that last night. We weren't together again."

"What about our baby?"

"I don't know. You were strong, so the baby probably lived, but that's a guess."

"We never saw each other again? Don't you know what happened to our lives? To our child?"

"My only memories are of us together. I have no memory of living beyond our last night. That may be why we're here. Unfinished business. To say goodbye."

Quame touched her hand, kissed her cheek, then was no more.

* * *

The sun blazed through the window, waking Krista.

103

Momentary sun blindness cleared as she recalled the night's experience. She hastily dressed in her running clothes and jogged toward the mansion.

After stopping to kick the fountain, she found Aunt Sheila in what had once been the mansion's dining room, sitting alone, drinking coffee.

"This is too much humidity for me," Aunt Sheila said as the dripping wet Krista entered, "And I live in this area." Aunt Sheila was sitting at a long dining table with several binders in front of her. "Krista, you should know I'm not an overly religious person, but this morning the Lord woke me up saying that you needed some help. He told me to get these books and papers and show them to you."

Krista knew the binders. They had been the highlight of the family reunion and her contribution to family lore—the annual financial records maintained by the plantation owners during the antebellum; financial documents containing the names, age, and value of the plantation inventory. She had found them while researching another project, but had never had any genuine interest in them until recently. Assembled by student interns, she had them copied, bound, and gifted them to Aunt Sheila.

Now, she couldn't wait to get her hands on them. An inventory of enslaved people was within the binders.

Quame had mentioned waiting two hundred years— 1820. She was lucky. The 1820 ledger was near the top, legible, and listed names. Among them was a Quame aged 18 valued at $790 and sold to Lemuel Swan for $820 in August.

She didn't see Krista. She looked for names close to Krista. Next, she looked for ages. A record from December 1820 listed three sixteen-year-old females –Venus, Alice, and Sistah. Sistah, valued at $600, had a two-month-old baby boy valued at $100. *Found you!*

Looking for Sistah in 1821, she was not so lucky. There was no Sistah, but there was a transaction of $800 for the sale of a female cook, aged 17. A 15-month-old baby appeared with a woman named Lula, aged forty-two.

Sistah sold, but not the baby?

Aunt Sheila had been quiet while Krista made her discovery. Handing her a Bible, she said, "Open it. The Lord says it's yours."

"A folded piece of paper fell out. Where did you find this?"

"One of your cousins found the paper sticking from underneath a bench and stuck in a jar. It was in the old part of the garden. He found it on a visit right after your folks died and gave it to me. I saved it in this old family Bible. If you look inside, there are births and deaths recorded from before the Civil War until the 1940s.

"The Lord was real chatty this morning. He wanted to make sure you got it today." Aunt Sheila rose from the table. "The name on the front of the letter is Quame. The name inside the letter should have been your name. The first girl in every generation has that name. Your mama decided to give you something fancier. I'll leave you alone now." Aunt Sheila walked away.

Krista opened the Bible first. There was a note on the back of the front cover.

"I have tried to record our family history from memory and family stories. I hope someone continues this after I'm gone. Mary Louis, 1910."

Krista turned the page to see a listing of births and deaths. She zoomed on the neatly penned names and dates that filled in her narrative.

Mama Lou   B. ??? D. 1865
Quame   B. 1802? D. 1821
Sistah   B. 1804 D. 1823
Jimmy (Quame) Louis   B. 1820 D.

Many other names and dates, many of them with the last name of Louis, some of which she recognized. She would explore the ancestors later. But, for now, Krista held the Bible, wondering why Quame and Sistah died shortly after being separated. *They no longer had each other for protection.*

She slowly opened the paper addressed to Quame.

I named our boy after you. He's called Jimmy by the massa. He is beautiful and strong. He walks and talks some. He misses you. So, do I.

I am gone run tomorrow. I need to find you. Little Quame is with Mama Lou. She loves him and will take good care of him. We can come back for him after I find you.

Nobody knows where you was sent. I heard somebody who looked like you died from the pox way down south. I don't think that is right. I still feel your spirit. I am hiding this letter near our special place. I know you will look there if you come back. Get our boy so we can raise him to be smart and strong. Try to find me. Quame, please. I love you.
Sistah

He never found the letter or his son, but as she had begged, he'd *finally* found her.

 After a successful career as an urban planning executive, RoseMary Covington Morgan has taken on a new challenge as an author.

Born in St. Louis, Missouri, she started creating stories. Her interest followed her through high school, to the University of Missouri, Columbus and Washington University, St. Louis.

RoseMary has published four short stories, *The Song* in the anthology *Storytellers: Tales from the Rio Vista Writers' Group, School Shopping, 'Twas, and My Big Red Shadow* in the Northern California Publishers and Authors (NCPA) anthology publications and two poems in NCPA publications.

She currently lives in Elk Grove, CA.

YELLOWSTONE:
THE BEAUTY AND THE BEASTS
LOREN DIAZ

I t was July 17th, 1984, day eighteen of our epic trip, the kind of trip that never fades from memory no matter how many years roll by. Our bicycles were laden with gear, packed in panniers and efficiently distributed, straddling front and rear wheels. Our sleeping bags and pads were strapped on the rear rack. Handlebar bags held our maps, wallets, riding gear, and snacks. We were riding east to west, Maryland to California, but not a direct path. Instead, our sights were set on several national parks along the journey. I had graduated from college in June and was to report for my first day of work at UL Labs in Santa Clara on August 18th, my first job as an electrical engineer. Until then, I would be free-roaming across America on my bicycle with two of my closest childhood friends, Donny and Mark.

Twenty-one hundred miles into our adventure, we had crossed through ten states and enjoyed many amazing sites of the beautiful American countryside. For the past ten days our ride was across the plains of Illinois, Iowa, Nebraska, and much of Wyoming. Each day was unique and invigorating. Riding through that part of the country gave me a whole new perspective on the vastness and wide-open space of the middle of America. We rode about one hundred and twenty-five miles each day, passing through only a handful of small towns, taking in this view of our country. The roads were smooth and straight, with gradual grades and the unfortunate, constant headwinds. Endless fields of wheat and corn were always in motion with the wind. I enjoyed sightings of livestock grazing and horses playing. It felt like we shared the roads with more farm equipment than cars as we pressed westward.

The previous day was the transition day when the Rocky Mountains came into full view in front of us. Earlier in the day, from our far-off distance, they appeared massive and close, like I could reach out and touch them. The sky was noticeably clear as we rode throughout the morning, marveling as the mountains seemed to grow as they came into sharper focus. Early that afternoon we rode into Cody, Wyoming. Cody was our doorstep to Yellowstone Park. We restocked food supplies and, with four hours of daylight left, continued toward the east entrance of the park.

That afternoon it was as though we melted into the Rockies. Cycling the forty-five miles, and with a two-thousand-foot elevation gain from Cody, we climbed through the steep, rocky canyons and along soft flowing meadows carved out over thousands of years by the North Fork of the Shoshone river. A couple of miles short of the east gate, we pulled off the highway and hiked with our bikes down to the river. It was long after sunset, and we needed the last light of day to set camp near the river. It grew chilly as the sky turned dark, and brought with it a cool, crisp breeze that we had not experienced on our trip until then. That night we hung our food up high for the first time as we were now in bear country. I had never slept so soundly as I did on that night. It might have been the low roar of the river and the chirping of the camel crickets, or the exhaustion of the one hundred and thirty miles we covered that day. I slept deeply, motionless on the soft natural bedding provided by the trees.

* * *

I awoke breathing in the frigid air and the strong incense of the mountain. As I opened my eyes, lying there under the trees in my bag, I needed a moment to recall where I was. The sky was just beginning to show signs of morning through its violet hues. The air, fresh and clear, carried the welcoming scent of pine trees. The sounds of river rambling over rocks and the light breeze through the trees gave me a satisfying feeling of accomplishment. We were now officially in the Rocky Mountains! Today we would ride through Yellowstone Park and camp in the park overnight before riding out the west entrance the following morning. The day also offered a change of pace and needed rest with frequent breaks and short hikes through the geyser basins. We were only covering seventy miles on the bikes. For me, more so than my cycling companions, this day was a highly anticipated part of my adventure. Both Mark and Donny had been to Yellowstone with their families on vacation, but it was my first time. I had done my research on Yellowstone before we left and was anticipating the diverse wildlife, amazingly beautiful vistas, and crowds of tourists in cars on the roads.

The next morning, we packed up and were on our bikes just as the sun was coming up over the lower hills behind us. My sights set on enjoying several major attractions, I felt like I had as a kid on my first visit to Disneyland. At the east entrance gate, we waited in the short car line to pay the fee and pick up our maps. The ranger gave us advice for keeping our food safe from the critters in the park, and we were on our way. Ascending to the rim of the Yellowstone basin, we set a strong pace, climbing fifteen hundred feet over the ten miles to Sylvan Pass. We stopped only to raise our arms in victory and take pictures before coasting effortlessly down into the heart of Yellowstone Park.

The highway led us down from the pass and we were peddling again as we skirted the north shore of Yellowstone Lake. Our first planned stop was for breakfast at the Fishing Bridge Museum and Visitor Center on the lake. At the visitor center, in addition to the videos about the history of the area and the ecosystem of the lake, we watched the requisite videos about how to be safe in the park around the geysers and hot pools, and when observing the larger animals such as bison, moose, and even bear. Bison are prolific throughout the park, and the safety video showed a dramatic scene of a bison goring and throwing a man who had ventured too close with his camera. There were many warnings in that video, "don't go near the bison," "bison are extremely strong and dangerous animals," "bison will charge humans," "bison can spin around quickly, accelerate fast, and jump high fences," and "bison can run thirty-five miles per hour." Though surprised by the examples of their strength and speed, I was really looking forward to the chance of spotting them in the park. Setting off from Fishing Bridge we turned left, continuing on the highway called the Grand Loop of Yellowstone. Our next stop was to experience the amazing geyser field on the shore of the lake in West Thumb.

The rest of that day was a very lazy pace with several stops over the thirty-five miles to our next camp. From West Thumb we enjoyed the leisurely ride to Old Faithful. The Grand Loop Highway crossed the continental divide twice on this leg, each time a celebration for us. The vistas out across the lush hillsides and valleys from those high points were spectacular. We saw dark spots moving in the distant meadows – our first sighting of bison. So far away, they seemed small and placid. At Old Faithful we toured the visitor center and then sat in the bleachers and watched Old Faithful erupt in all its glory. We also hiked the elaborate boardwalk trails throughout this geyser basin. The delicate golden meadows and crystal blue steaming hot pools were amazing. We splurged for a lunch in the lodge restaurant and then prepared for our next ride up to the Fountain Paint Pots trailhead. Later, hiking through that area, I was again amazed at the natural wonders of Yellowstone. Vibrant shades of reds, yellows and browns gurgled and belched at our feet. Brilliant colored mud created by iron oxidation, mixed and bubbled up from the deep cracks.

Back on the bikes for our final leg to the campgrounds, and about halfway to our destination, we came upon a line of cars stopped on the highway. The road at this point was only two lanes, one in each direction, and narrow, with little paved shoulder. There was no oncoming traffic and the road ahead bent to the right following the hillside. It would have been dangerous to use the oncoming lane to pass cars, so we fell in line and then slowly continued passing the stopped cars using the right shoulder to move up toward the front. I was riding in the lead of our group and a minute later was in a panic.

After passing a half dozen cars I looked up to see a bison walking straight toward us on the shoulder about twenty yards ahead. The drop-off and then a hill on our right did not look inviting, so in that split second, I made the only move possible, slipping in between two stopped cars, a sedan in front and a small motor home behind, with about five feet between.

I maneuvered between the two cars, planning to escape on the other side in the empty oncoming lane, but came to an abrupt stop. I stopped breathing too. Three more bison were walking parallel with the one on the shoulder, but in the oncoming lane. Had I not stopped quick enough I might have bumped into the closest one.

At that same moment Donny and Mark came in behind me, bumping and pushing their way into that tight space just as the bison were passing us on the left and right. I saw the panicked look on their faces and was certain the noise we were making would also gain the attention of the bison.

We were penned in with no escape other than to climb onto a car. I exhaled as the bison strolled past, as I was within arm's length of the nearest one. With a strangely oversized head and large dark eyes, they smelled of strong musk and damp earth. I listened to their grunts and snorts as they passed. It was curious to see the thick wool fur on their back, light, but darker underneath, shedding off in chunks.

In a moment they had passed having shown no interest in our panicked escape. The oncoming cars followed a short distance behind the three bison, and the car line in front of us began breaking up. In the car ahead, a young boy in the backseat was looking back and giving us a wave, a wide smile on his face.

A short while later, still energized from our encounter with the bison, we descended to a valley and across the Madison River. The long meadow with the river snaking through it looked like a paradise. Our campground would be off to the left a short way down the meadow.

Crossing the bridge over the river, we slowed, following the gaze of tourists standing on the shoulder. Bison, a small head of fifteen or twenty a couple of hundred yards to the east, were grazing on the lush with green and golden grasses along the river. I slowed to take in the spectacular view as the river valley, reflecting the setting sun, extended for what seemed like a mile, both east and west of the bridge.

We checked into the group campsite for backpackers and cyclists, still with plenty of daylight to set camp and enjoy the meadow before dark. It had been both a serene and harrowing day.

This campsite was situated at the far end of a large campground, on the edge of the meadow west of the bridge. The view of the meadow was spectacular. We befriended another group of riders that had already set their camp and learned from them there were hot springs that we could relax in over at the river. They pointed us to a trail that would lead us straight to one, only about a three-minute hike.

Excited to sit in a hot pool, we secured our food bag in the bear box, changed quickly, and set out on the trail. I marveled at the amazing views in this meadow in the late afternoon light. The contrast between the lush golden meadow and the dark tree-studded mountains at the far edge rising sharply to the sky was stark. Off in the distance I could see that cars were stopped along the bridge, no doubt watching the bison grazing.

The hot spring was perched near the edge of the river. It was up on the bank, carved out as a round crater eroded into the meadow, a constant supply of warm water flowing up within the crater forming a shallow pool that drained to the river. The water level was a couple of feet down from the rim of the crater, and we climbed down and eventually settled in, stretched out so that only our heads were above the water line and resting on the bank.

The air was pungent with the smell and taste of sulfur rising from the spring. Warm but not hot, the water felt smooth and silky, almost velvety between my fingers. We were comparing stories from the day, relaxed and untroubled, and at some point, I nodded off. I awoke sharply when kicked in the leg. Disoriented at first, I sat up looking across the pool to Donny and Mark. They both looked as if they had just seen a ghost and Mark was motioning me to lower myself back down. I laid back and a moment later I felt the ground vibrating underneath me.

Simultaneously, the sky above grew dark. A huge dark creature appeared from nowhere, straight above, and it felt as if it were passing over me. As in a slow-motion dream, I could see each step, the bottom of the hoofs, the large swaying head and belly as the bison stepped past our spring and I could see the dust scatter above me where a hoof met the ground.

As if on a tightrope strung along the edge of the crater, it passed unbelievably close to where my head lay. I again could hear the grunts and snorts and smell their strong musk over the sulfur. The beast had passed by and with my heart pounding I sat up knowing I had somehow cheated death. Mark again raised a hand motioning me to hold perfectly still. I immediately knew what that meant and not wanting to tempt fate a second time, I quickly maneuvered myself around to the other side of the spring as the next bison strolled by on the same path.

The three of us sat there in awe, motionless, while the entire herd moved past us. Only one more bison chose the path up against the edge of our spring as the rest were walking further off in the meadow. A couple of minutes later we climbed out of the crater, survivors, staring across the meadow at a line of onlookers stretched along the edge of the campground. A handful of them waited for our arrival across the meadow to hear our story. We told it more than once that evening as word spread around the campsite.

Later in the darkness, after cleaning our dishes and all the stories had been retold, I settled into my sleeping bag. Lying there, I remembered our time spent at the Fishing Bridge visitor center that morning. I thought about the videos and the warnings. What should we have done differently? The close-up views of the bison, feeling their massive size, smelling their musty fur, hearing their grunts and snorts, and looking them directly in the eye, are all imprints in my memory forever.

As I was drifting off to sleep, I remembered the final warning, the one at the end of the video, and that will be my warning to others who are headed to Yellowstone for a vacation, the one that was almost our fatal mistake, "Once you allow yourself to get too close to a bison, there is no escape."

 Loren Diaz is a retired Electrical Engineer, a husband, a father, and an aspiring writer. An avid reader of American and European murder mysteries, he most enjoys those that showcase and intertwine both the harsh and serene landscapes with diverse cultures and history of the areas. A new member to NCPA, he was born and raised in the San Francisco Bay Area and cursed with an appetite for adventure. In retirement he is working on his Spanish language skills, writing, looking forward to more time for travel with family, and always scheming his next adventure.

THE BEAUTIFUL POWER OF PECAN ROLLS

DANIEL SCHMITT

Cal died six years ago from diabetes complications. We first met while bartending at the Reubens Restaurant in La Mesa, California in 1973. No one would have predicted that our initial encounter as bartenders would grow into a lifelong friendship that lasted until his death.

We were both in our early twenties, but two more different people could hardly have existed. Cal was on the fast-track to everywhere. The son of a career Air Force Master Sergeant, Cal was well travelled, had lived in numerous countries, and spoke German. His school-teaching mother taught him the piano and guitar. Cal attended high school in Southern California where he played football and baseball, was student body president, and graduated at the top of his class academically. He was attending San Diego State University when we first met, and during his four years there, he was student body president and graduated with a degree in Political Science. The next year, Cal went on to U.C. Berkeley where he attained a law degree and an MBA.

I grew up in the small north-central Wisconsin town of Schofield and hardly strayed from there until the age of 19 when the military came a-knocking. I graduated from high school BARELY, much preferring to spend my time fishing and hunting rather than hitting the books. After my military service, I decided that higher education was the way to go, but it took me a full seven years to earn my degree and teaching credential.

Our decades-long friendship began while working

together in that Rueben's bar, but it quickly strengthened with our mutual infatuation with motorcycles, our macabre senses of humor, and our fondness for food. I suppose, as much as anything, it was that love of food, specifically pecan rolls, that was instrumental in binding our futures together.

During part of our bartending days, Cal and I roomed together. A few times each year, my mother would mail me a couple of tins of her knock-your-socks off homemade pecan rolls. Cal enjoyed these postal delights as much as I did, and with every pecan roll devoured, he'd smack his lips, shake his head, and utter, "Wow, Dan, these are great!" It got so I would have to hide one of the tins from Cal lest he consume all the rolls in one sitting. Cal begged me to get Mom's recipe, so he could make the pecan rolls himself, but that was impossible because Mom didn't have a written recipe; she made most of her baked goods from memory.

Almost every summer in those days, I would spend a week or so with my family in Wisconsin, taking in the Marathon County Fair, visiting old high school friends, and doing some serious walleye fishing. I believe it was the summer of 1976 when the incident occurred. It just so happened that same summer Cal had decided to quit his bartending job and spend a couple of months selling bibles door to door in Detroit, Michigan.

Early on in our friendship, I had come to see Cal as an enigma shrouded in a thick blanket of San Diego marine fog. Just when I thought I had him figured out, BAMMM, he'd hit me with something so totally unexpected and out of character I was left wondering if I knew the guy at all. Given Cal's penchant for religious irreverence, his plan to sell bibles was one of those BAMMM moments.

Selling bibles that summer was Cal's plan, and when he heard I'd be in Wisconsin at the same time, he told me, "Hey, Dan, I'll fly over for a few days, and you can show me around your hometown. I've never been to Wisconsin." Cal wasn't the kind of guy who asked permission for anything; he just told you what he planned to do, and I knew it would have been fruitless to try to talk him out of it.

The day I got home, the only home I'd ever known until

I left for the military in 1967, I mentioned to my mother that a friend would be visiting for a few days, and she was delighted. During the days before Cal arrived, Mom excitedly told all the neighbors that "Danny's best friend from California was coming to visit!"

That day arrived, and I picked up Cal at the Central Wisconsin Airport. My mother, father, sister, and younger brothers were in the kitchen when the two of us came through the back door. I promptly introduced Cal, "Mom, Dad, this is my best friend Cal."

After a few seconds of uncomfortable silence, my mother said in a rather unconvincing manner, "Nice to meet 'cha, Cal. Danny, why don't you show Cal his bedroom?" While Cal was unpacking, I came back into the kitchen. Silence hung throughout the room. Mom looked at me and whispered, "Danny, he's black! What are the neighbors gonna say? Why didn't you tell me you were bringing a black man home?"

Truth be told, very few people of color had ever stepped foot in north-central Wisconsin in those days, and I knew if I had told my mother Cal was black before his arrival, she wouldn't have said he couldn't come, but she would have spent lots of time worrying about the uncomfortable situation I had put her in. I looked at her and said, "Mom, just give Cal a chance. You'll love the guy. You'll see."

The next morning after breakfast, I told Cal I would be taking one of my younger brothers fishing on Lake Wausau. Cal looked at me in surprise and said, "Dan, dude, I don't fish. My dad fishes. I don't fish. What am I going to do?" After a short pause, he continued, "Hey, do you think your mother could show me how to make those pecan rolls?"

Well, if there was one thing Mother loved more than baking for Dad and us seven Schmitt kids, it was sharing her skills with others. So, even though she laid awake most of the night worrying herself sick and was still quite anxious that morning about having a black man in her house, her eyes lit up at the opportunity to share with Cal the secrets to her famous pecan rolls. My younger brother Mike and I grabbed a couple of fishing poles and a tackle box from the

119

basement and headed out the door, with Mom and Cal putting on aprons in preparation for the hours-long process of making pecan rolls.

After a full morning of fishing, Mike and I walked the three blocks back home. The two people working on those pecan rolls, one an expert, one a novice, represented two very different worlds, but both Mother and Cal loved to laugh, and as Mike and I approached the backyard, we could hear loud howling coming from the kitchen. We opened the back door, and there were the two bakers at the table kneading the dough. Now, anyone who has ventured into pastry making knows that a fair amount of flour is necessary during the kneading process, and there stood Mom with a smattering of flour on her apron, but it was Cal who caught our attention. Cal looked like a ghost with flour covering him head to foot, and Mom had tears rolling down her face laughing.

So, the ice was broken over the making of those pecan rolls, but it substantially thawed once they were out of the oven. Cal kept going back for more and more and more, and, in true character and with setting having no bearing on expressing his delight, with every roll devoured he would smack his lips, shake his head and utter, "Wow, Mrs. Schmitt, these are great!" Mother was absolutely in her glory that my California friend loved her pecan rolls.

Over the next few days until Cal flew back to Detroit, we showed him around our small town, went bowling at Coral Lanes and took him to a Friday fish fry at the VFW Hall. Everywhere we went, Mom couldn't wait to introduce "Danny's best friend from California" to people she knew. She even came along to see him off when I took Cal to the airport.

Mom had a habit of calling me about mid-November each year to ask if I would be coming home for Christmas. When her call came that year, we talked about the family and new things going on in our lives. Then, the expected question came, "Danny, are ya coming home this Christmas?" Before I could answer, she followed with, "Do ya think Cal could come home with ya?"

Daniel Schmitt is a retired English and social science teacher who has been dabbling with his own writing for the better part of forty years.

His writing inspirations are from personal experiences like travelling, hiking, and simply observing the world and people around him. He usually writes short pieces and especially enjoys recounting some of his youthful experiences while growing up in north-central Wisconsin.

Writing, like reading, constantly opens his mind to new experiences and ways of thinking, and brings him lots of enjoyment.

UP FOR A RIDE?

A.K. BUCKROTH

The large decision to move, to go away, to get out, gave my husband and I the shared passions of travelling. Our dog would be embraced in this decision. Getting in the car and going. Our physical years, tainted with aches and pains, would not hold us back. The aching stiffness of arthritis being a factor in each of us would not dissuade this decision. Freedom is a highway!

Therefore, my husband's and my dream of driving cross country – to literally re-locate in the State of Virginia – came to fruition.

Cash, our totally white, long-haired Parsons Terrier had recently tallied his twelfth birthday. Adopted at the age of three months, his existence easily filled our empty nest. His slower running and jumping abilities became enhanced with a soft, chewable, once-a-day "happy joint" tablet. They worked! Hmm. I often wondered if I should chew and swallow one of these tablets. However, running and jumping at my age seem laughable!

Family members residing in Virginia called to us: a daughter, a daughter-in-law, two very young grandchildren and numerous relatives and friends dotted along the East Coast of the United States from Maine to Florida. Also, the intrigue of a lower cost of living became a greatly rewarding thought; baby-sitting along with tutoring the grand babies, bonding would become memorable for all involved!

No other reasons or rationale would be necessary. *We're doing it! We're going*!

Before the Sacramento house was placed on the 2021 "sellers' market," I signed up with two leading online real estate companies: Zillow and MLS. Two real estate agents were contacted – one to sell the California property, the other to share a 'virtual tour' for a Virginia property.

Do not doubt the numerous tasks to consider before hiring real estate agents in each of the two states. Final escrow has important requirements to foster peace of mind: inspection reports; fixing what needed to be fixed; change of address forms; hiring a moving/hauling company; yard sales; purging; packing, and then, wait for it ... more packing. Quality time spent with numerous friends became all important. They were made aware of this five-year dream/plan that turned into seven years.

Overwhelmed with the physical and emotional chaos of this decision, the last of three vehicles became packed with a canvas sack belted to its roof and our dog's bed comfortably spread on a portion of the back seat. I thought of the similarities of the Conestoga wagon days in the 1800s, having to cross this continent. Courage became an important factor.

Due to the continuation of the viral pandemic and its worsening increase of lives lost as televised in the southern states at this time, we chose to drive the northern route across the United States.

Vaccinated and boosted, peace of mind existed with our numerous facial masks, cleansing cloths and hand washes. "Social distancing" would remain a constant determinant.

When the California house sold, we had to leave. We had no place to go but forward.

It was 59°F when leaving the state at noontime on January 5th, 2022. The odometer read 95,495 as we began the designated route to Virginia. My husband as the main driver, my co-piloting skills involved keeping track of map locations; supplying snacks and refreshments from the back seat cooler; listening to Cash's breathing as he hunkered in the back seat; reporting the sights to include cows, horses and/or sheep; searching for hotels in each locale; calling for pet-friendly room reservations; whatever else may have been required.

Exiting CA on I-80, we passed through beloved towns and cities such as historical Auburn, Lincoln, Placerville,

Newcastle, Grass Valley, and others. Reassured memories of repeated visits to each city flooded our hearts and minds. For instance, Lincoln features some of the best entrepreneurial thrift and consignment shops I had ever entered. Its downtown area carries the scents of freshly baked quiche in one place, cupcakes in another, or homemade eateries, each neighboring the other.

Placerville and Newcastle were home to fresh garden vegetables for purchase. I often favored freshly laid eggs along with the purchase of butternut squash, the "purple-est" of purple eggplants and a cabbage the size of a basketball. Truly.

The city of Colfax, California, with its rocky terrain held a favorite memory of gold-panning. Yes indeed! Just like in the 1800s, my husband and I had borrowed equipment to accomplish this adventurous task in the fast flowing, deliciously clear Bunch Creek.

Requirements included a deep plastic pan with a ridged bottom plate designed specifically for gold panning, some small glass vials to store our gold find, a fine strainer, and a picnic lunch of homemade egg salad sandwiches and tall thermoses of ice water.

At one point, I had meandered into the fast-flowing creek, knee-deep, to splash the cold water on my face and arms. It nicely refreshed my skin. We had not only appreciated the continuous, melodious sounds of the creek's steady flow, but after six hours, a very small portion of each vial held gold chips.

Continuing on to Reno, Nevada, memories of a friends' daughter's wedding became a fond recollection:

* * *

Never having been there before, and not having seen the parents of the bride for a long time, we had looked forward to this trip.

Keep in mind, there are seventeen different mountain ranges in Reno. I did not know which we had to traverse to get to the final destination, but we got there with a trusty set of snow tire chains.

After finding a parking spot and removing the tire chains, we had to cautiously walk through a foot of snow on that early March afternoon in 2006. Departing the warmth of the Sacramento Valley, the snow had been unexpected. Our fancy attire did not include snow boots or heavy jackets so we had to make the best with what we had. All in all, the wedding became a lovely affair, of course, with the pink champagne a concoction of unending and laughable bubbles. After a time, I believe these bubbles warmed my toes.

* * *

But for now, the dirty, snow-bordered interstate of Nevada became drab and boring. I picked up my book regarding different lifestyles and continued reading. After having completed two chapters, we quietly passed through Sparks, Nevada at 10:15-ish AM, on our way to Winnemucca, Nevada.

Just past Winnemucca, we put $39.50 worth of gas in the tank to fill it because areas of rest, food, and sleep were few and far between. Never having heard of Winnemucca, the name itself had awakened my attention. Winnemucca lies in a valley surrounded by peaceful-looking snow-covered peaks. Stepping out of the car at the station, I did a 360° look-about to view this awe-inspiring landscape. Its cold air tasted clean. We were made aware that soon, more freezing temperatures would be upon us. For instance, 8°F in Northeastern Nevada would grow into a whopping 28°F later.

The car's bright red "engine light" beeped. It displayed itself on the dashboard. Its relentless brightness frightened us. Rather than chance it, we left the Interstate and circled back to Winnemucca to search for an automotive retailer.

Finding one, we inquired at the sales counter, but the clerk strongly suggested that this problem sounded like "the fuel pump needed to be replaced. There is a dealership in town that would take care of this problem for you. We do not carry fuel pumps here."

Dealership?! Arrgghh! And *uh-oh*! I have always found the term 'dealership' to be frightening in and of itself! Intimidating. To be avoided at all costs!

A different retailer suggested we buy a "Code Reader." The husband called a mechanic friend in California who agreed. Doing so, my husband plugged it under the dash board near the steering column. That looked easy enough and it read the fuel pump needed assistance. Holy _____!!

In total denial of this quandary, refusing to face the expense of a dealership or trip delay, I opened the glove compartment and pulled out the automobile's glossy informational book. Looking up this problem, I found that the gas tank cover could be improperly placed. It was.

Holy moly! With a quick opening and closing of the fuel tank's cover, the red engine light went out, gone. Yay me! So simple a fix. Thank goodness I kept that book!

Problem solved, but it was late, so we checked into the *Winners Casino Hotel* in Winnemucca at 7:00PM. My husband and I were able to get Cash settled before we wandered off to the casino for dinner. The menu advertised homemade entrees that appealed to our appetites. For instance, a favored vegetable omelet for dinner with sourdough toast one day, a platter of spaghetti and meatballs for lunch the next day, and a Reuben sandwich at one point helped to energize us.

The bright and colorful flashing lights of the casino invited us to walk about its hall and play a couple of one-penny slot machines each. After a half hour, I walked away with $2.70; my husband with a whopping $7.20. We were happy.

Cash delighted in the separate "grass and dirt dog area" close to the parking lot. The roadside rest stops did not allow him, or any dog, to run freely, of course. Ten minutes of this type of happiness in freezing temperatures made a large difference in his attitude. After having been in a moving vehicle for hours at a time and having to refamiliarize himself with different motel/hotel rooms each night, his happiness made us happy.

Due to the cold, I wore my midi-length lined coat, a knit cap and gloves, while Cash remained covered in his multi-colored doggy sweater. His swift wagging tail and open-mouthed smile told me he was happy after each walk. This is always a good thing. His collar and leash, food and water bowl, along with a small sack of kibble and his favorite beefy treats, were easily accessible to us. A pleasant two-night stay here refreshed our minds and bodies.

We didn't start the car in those two days. Breathing steadily, we remained onward bound. Goodbye Winnemucca, Nevada. Salt Lake City, Utah, here we come.

Back on the road, the Great Salt Lake Desert greeted us inside the border. To me it appeared rather unappealing. The numerous acres for which it was called remained dry, tannish white in color, flat, looking salty. Very different. Unhealthy. Not a lake at all. It bore no water. It appeared purposeless. No signs of life.

Darkness fell upon us as we arrived at the outskirts of Salt Lake City. The city lights in this unfamiliar place glared at us. Neither of us could read the street signs. The highways, freeways and surface streets were overcrowded, too busy for us to attend to sign reading. Gasping as if hyperventilating, Cash told us he needed to get out of the car. Pulling into the University of Utah's expansive and well-lit parking lot, I took Cash out for at least a fifteen-minute walk while my husband used his cell phone to find a hotel. Three pees on two parking lot trees and one poo later, Cash nestled back into his car-comfort zone. We needed to hunker down. To chill. To eat. To sleep.

The Salt Lake City Hilton Hotel, at $130.00 per night with a one-time $75.00 pet charge, taxes not included, located a block behind us, had an available room.

Definitely *not* pet friendly for that price, and over our agreed upon hotel allowance, but we had no place else to go, with our over-exhausted minds. We were given a third-floor room at the end of a 100-foot-long carpeted hallway leading into a room with two queen size beds.

Cash became jittery inside the elevator, this being his first ride. Looking at each of us bright-eyed, then staring at the door in breathless wonder, he jumped out as soon as the door opened. His pleasant personality returned when realizing solid ground was there. Many more opportunities brought him to have to ride the elevator. He did not care for any of them. However, bathroom breaks are important.

The beds became a pleasant resting place as we slunk under thick, fluffy white comforters. The softer-than-soft white down feathered pillows were a wonderful addition. A pleasant, deep sleep overcame each of us. As usual, Cash's car pillows were laid close to our bed. The physical amenities here became a two-day stay.

I continue to think of Salt Lake City as a spider's web, one that temporarily caught us in its web: many cross streets causing an excess of anxiety for a newcomer, along with traffic noise and the stiff and sticky scent of automobile fumes. Unwelcome. Unfriendly. Sure, directional street signs were everywhere which made our destination more confusing as we had no time to read them! Crazy. We hope to never have to be there again.

Checking out at 10AM on Sunday, January 9th, we headed toward Wyoming. Somewhere around our arrival at the Wyoming/Colorado/Nebraska border at 12:45 PM January 10th, we drove through the Continental Divide at 7,000 feet. My ears popped. Fluffy clouds surrounded acre upon acre of bare flatlands. An occasional, lonely looking farmhouse or an out building came into view. The ground frozen, I could barely see the tilling lines for supposed crops. 942 miles from Sacramento, we still had a way to go.

Close to the Nebraska/Wyoming border, I insisted we stop for a hot dog lunch at a place called "Fat Dogs." I bought the last two hot dogs that were readily available – with warmed buns, of course. Pasting ketchup, sweet green relish, and spicy brown mustard on each, I also grabbed two 18-liter bottles of electrolyte water. Yum. Cash was given a soft, chewy dog treat with a small bowl of water, becoming satisfied for the time being.

Still on I-80 Nebraska, we headed for the Quality Inn sign we saw from the interstate. At 4PM, the warm rays of the sun being a continual imposter of the true temperature,

I had to remind myself that January has always been one of the coldest times of the year no matter where I was on this continent, except maybe Miami, Florida. The temperature this day did not reach above 37°F.

The parking lot of this motel had not been thoroughly cleared of snow and ice. This first impression was not good. Remnants of light brown sand mixed with the once pure white snow made the area look dingy, deserted without other cars. I mentally accepted that we would get a room along with negative consequences. Pet friendly, the $84.00 per night would be acceptable.

All in all, the room appeared to be clean. However, I performed my usual thorough sweep of the bed looking for bed bugs, dirt, whatever; the bathroom area appeared clean holding bleached white towels and an extra roll of toilet paper. Important stuff. The noisy metal wall heater could be heard jangling as it warmed the room. I became grateful. This room would be okay for one night. Oh yes, the sheets smelled of bleach which is always a good sign to me. Clean and fresh.

After getting acquainted with the hotel's outdoor surroundings — specifically a doggy area — the Virginia real estate woman gave us a call. She seemed very excited about having found us a house in Chesapeake, Virginia contingent upon our requests: three bedrooms, two baths, no stairs, on a quarter of an acre, in suburbia. Goodness knew that we needed a place to go! So, we agreed to partake in a "virtual tour" with her via our cell phones. This quaint parcel seemed perfect via the telephone screens. We made a bid. Located in *Chesapeake Downs*, Virginia, our plans to meet in person were scheduled.

Gosh, we became quiet assimilating these facts. So much happening so fast, our heads were spinning.

Back in the car on January 11, 2022, we left the 'quality' of Nebraska skirting the border of Iowa via I-80 toward Missouri. We became reacquainted with black ice and saw a white Mercedes Sedan in a ditch below. We heeded that warning by slowing down to 55 MPH from 70 MPH. Good thing, too. Not two miles from that scene, a tractor trailer lay on its side.

Our next stop for gas at $2.85 per gallon easily filled the tank. We continued, becoming somewhat feverish with excitement at the thought of actually putting a monetary bid on a home under such uncommon and unusual circumstances.

This is part of one of the 'new world actions' caused by the onslaught of COVID-19.

A Denny's restaurant outside Indiana became a welcome respite for a much-needed warm meal. Cash enjoyed a brisk and relieving walk before gobbling his bowl of kibble in the parking lot. The steady late afternoon temperature of 45+°F slowly lowered as the sun began to set.

The sunset combined two shades of light blue with pink stripes dotted with wispy white clouds, helping to reflect our happy moods.

Into Kentucky, I no longer paid attention to the highway street names. I was tired. I wanted this to end. I wanted to see the Chesapeake house. The Great Plains of America were blank...nothing growing, nothing specific or special to see. Not on a touring venue by any means, my husband and dog and I were on a mission … to prosper in Virginia.

A jumble of routes beginning with I-80 onto I-29, I-70, I-435, I-77 and I-64 into West Virginia, a quick interim somewhere in between, we made no time to stop, West Virginia became the quickest drive-through ever! I-64 brought us into Virginia, finally. *Welcome to Virginia!*

No more being a co-pilot! No more having to check mattresses for bed bugs, no more having to listen to the rattle of a hotel wall heater, no more listening to voices on a shared wall, no more worries about the car, the dog, the husband, the self and the wallet, we arrived in Virginia. Chesapeake, Virginia.

CA -> NV -> UT -> WY -> CO -> NE -> IA -> MO -> IL -> IN -> KY -> WV -> VA. Whew!

Amen!

 A.K. Buckroth is presently a member of Northern California Publishers and Authors (NCPA), Sacramento Suburban Writers Club (SSWC), and the San Joaquin Valley Writers (SJVW). Once obtaining a Master's Degree from the University of Phoenix, she gained the empowerment and knowledge to write her first book.

Known as a "Professional Diabetic", Ms. Buckroth has maintained more than six decades with this disease. Read it all in *My Diabetic Soul – An Autobiography* Revised Edition © *2018*, which brought her numerous awards.

She is also responsible for three other books: *Me and My Dog Named Money…a child's story of diabetes* (Revised © 2019), *Me & My Money Too Book Two* (Revised © 2019), and *Kisses for Cash…T1D meets T2D Book Three* © 2016, which received an NCPA award.

Available via Amazon, Kindle, Nook, Smashwords and Audio.com among others. More information via www.mydiabeticsoul.com and #buckroth.

Email address: mydiabeticsoul@gmail.com

ODE TO SEA RANCH

PATRICIA E. CANTERBURY

During the late 1980s to the mid 1990s various members of my writing critique group would spend the long three-day weekend, once called *Columbus Day Holiday Weekend,* in a rental at the tiny ocean village of Sea Ranch off the Pacific Coast Highway.

Our *road trip,* which depending on traffic, was approximately an hour or two drive from Sacramento, and we would arrive at Ethel's home immediately after breakfast, parking our cars in her driveway. We'd be ready for the trip to Guerneville where we would stop for lunch. Along the way we would settle in, always with Ethel at the wheel, me riding shotgun, and whoever the other two writers joining us were, would be in the back.

I can't remember if I was chosen for the shotgun spot because I was the only native Californian, or because I'm the bossiest.

It didn't matter, we got lost *every year.*

We'd head west on Interstate 80 until we reached the Napa turnoff. In the early years before many of the onion fields were plowed under, we could tell when we were getting near our exit from the strong aroma of onions near the old Nut Tree settlement.

Turning right after we had driven about 30 miles plus or minus, past the Nut Tree, we got near the edge of Napa, where the odor of ripe grapes overtook the smell of onions.

Continuing across Sonoma County to the Interstate 101 exit, we'd head north to Petaluma. It didn't matter how many times we'd driven this particular route we always felt as if we were headed in the wrong direction from where we wanted to go.

Going up 101 *everyone* was on the lookout for the Petaluma exit. Now we were in *egg country,* with tiny farms full of range free chickens running wild.

We were only an hour away from San Francisco but we may have been on Mars as far as landscape went. We knew we were still in Northern California because everyone was still very, very friendly and outgoing.

And we, as usual, were lost.

As we eased through Petaluma, searching for the street which would take us to Guerneville, we were on high alert for the large church which was our clue to keep right and continue through the apple tree groves. If, God forbid, anything ever happened to that church we'd still be driving around trying to find our way west.

After many more miles we finally crossed an ancient bridge indicating we were near the Russian River which, depending on the year, might be low enough for us to walk across.

We had arrived in time for lunch on Guerneville's main street. After lunch and checking out the equally antique 5 and 10 cent store, probably built the same date as the bridge we'd crossed, the four of us stocked up on groceries at Safeway then continued to the Pacific coast, through the Armstrong Redwood State Reserve and up Highway 1, the Pacific Coast Highway.

It was always interesting to guess what or who we would pass on the narrow, two-lane windy road: sometimes bicyclists, racing to heaven knows where, or more than likely two or three cows which wandered on the road to get to the other side, near the ocean rocks!

Finally, we'd make it to Sea Ranch where we would spend the next two and half days at the same house we'd rented for the past ten or so Columbus weekends. The house had four bedrooms, three baths, a kitchen and dining room. Off the kitchen was a locked door that we didn't have a key to, and had just assumed it was for storage or other personal things.

We kept reading comments from previous guests about

the wonderful theater and abundance of movies, so when we returned the key after our first visit, we asked, "What theater?" And were told "Oh didn't you ask about the theater when you called?" Now, how would we know to ask if the house had a theater?

Unknown to us that first time we rented the house, the locked door led to a fully stocked movie theater filled with comfortable sofas and a large screen on which we could watch movies supplied by the home owner, who had eclectic tastes. Every year after that, we watched everything from the latest movies to vintage 1940s mysteries

We didn't have a clue we were missing a room, because of how all the neighboring houses were situated, and there wasn't a hell of a lot of space to notice this house was larger, since it was surrounded on three sides by large Monterey Pine. Plus, right near the carport were the dumpsters, which were constructed to keep raccoon and bears out of the garbage.

Another thing the rental agency didn't tell visitors was that one needed a degree in mechanical engineering to OPEN the dumpsters to *put the garbage* in. It took all four of us professional women trying the locks many times before we finally figured out how to open the dumpsters – once again proving four women were smarter than the average raccoon.

The deck had a magnificent view of the Pacific, which was beautiful first thing in the morning with the sun rising in the east hovering over the pines, and us hovering over coffee, biscuits, orange juice and eggs. Or us late at night with a glass or two of wine where we watched shooting stars and on one remarkable occasion, a UFO, which hovered just to the west of the house and was also observed by German tourists at the Sea Ranch restaurant. We searched the local newspapers once we returned home, but not one word was written about whatever it was all four of us, plus the Germans, had seen.

Speaking of night, the speed limit was set at 15 mph throughout Sea Ranch. What a laugh, if anyone could drive faster than 4 miles an hour after day one, they were lucky.

Jackrabbits ruled the night and NEVER let anyone, regardless of how large the car or van, think otherwise. They had that Dustin Hoffman manner about them: stomping their little feet, and one could almost hear them saying *"Hey...I'm walkin' here"*.

Several great things happened to us over the years while on vacation at Sea Ranch: Terris was able to complete the final draft of her award-winning mystery novel, Ethel discovered that two of her characters weren't who she thought they were, Ceola wrote wonderful poems about the sea and redwood trees, Geri wrote her first novel to acclaimed reviews, and I was able to design the layout for the town of Poplar Cove for my pre-teen/young adult historical fiction series.

Patricia E. (Pat) Canterbury is a native Sacramentan, political scientist, art collector, retired state administrator, author of seven novels and a world traveler.

Her Young Adult novel, *The Case of the Bent Spoke*, won Honorable Mention at the 2019 NCPA Awards. Pat's short stories have appeared in over 30 anthologies, including the 2018 Brom Stoker finalist, *Sycorax's Daughters.*
Pat and her elderly cat live in Sacramento.

Website www.patmyst.com email: patmyst@aol.com

The Busboy's Secret August 2021 – Obsidian Anthology
A Day in Havana – Destination World, Volume 2 NCPA Anthology
Omens, Medicine Men and Myths – Destination World, Volume 1 NCPA Anthology
The Case of the Bent Spoke: A Poplar Cove Mystery – 2019 NCPA Young Adult Honorable Mention
Sycorax's Daughter's 2018 Brom Stoker finalist – Anthology
The Geaha Incident: An Afro-Futuristic mystery
The Secret of Morton's End: A Poplar Cove Mystery
Carlotta's Secret: A Delta Mystery – optioned for a motion picture

AMERICAN CATS

ROBERTA "BERTA" DAVIS

Celeste cuddled her black cat as she carried him to their temporary abode in Lincoln. She entered an old cottage reminiscent of her home in England. "Here we are, Nacht sweetie. It's a bed and breakfast owned by a good friend.

Nacht wasn't paying much attention, too busy stretching and sniffing the cozy abode.

"My new friend, Telly, is paying us to do a story on America. It's not just one story, but she wants me to make training videos and lots of stories. This is big. I could pay off my bills and get more stuff for us. It's like a paid vacation!" Her voice softened, "Why does such a good deal feel so weird?"

Nacht wiggled as Celeste unfastened his harness, and trotted off to explore. There were many scents from plants, trees, and nearby creatures, so invigorating.

When Nacht rejoined her, Celeste had settled in the kitchen nook with a cup of tea and opened her laptop. "Let's see about this, Telly." She pulled up the website for a brunette, attractive, with purple streaks in her long, dark hair." Hmm, she's an animal rescue advocate, publisher of stories and movies… freelance pilot. Owns her own hover jet? Cool."

Nacht pawed at Telly's picture.

"Yes, she dresses funny. That cloak is something between retro and space fiction."

Celeste called Telly. "Hi, yeah, come on by. You'll see why I asked for this weekend for my story on America. The old town here is great and there's a Renaissance Faire within a few hours… No, we're not doing tourist traps. Your boss wants the real America, right? Okay. My friend owns this place. The catch is, I help her trap and release some feral kitties here. Maybe we can tame a few of them. Okay, see you."

Trapping a cat is almost as hard as herding cats. Celeste wouldn't bother trying just yet. She found a note left by the cottage owner, reading, "Hi Celeste, thanks so much for helping with the cats! I'll take care of them but we gotta get them fixed. Traps are in the patio, feeding station by the shed. Hugs, Skyla. Thank you, thank you!!" The traps already had a towel over each, and food. For now, Celeste put the traps near the shed with doors open and treats inside for the cats to inspect.

After lounging around and sharing chicken, Nacht and Celeste set out, kitty in his harness and leash, Celeste dressed for a hike. They took their rental car into town, where numerous people complimented Nacht for his casual bravery. Telly joined them, her curiosity clear as they explored local cafes and century-old buildings with diverse vendors, and dined in a big cafe with live music.

Surprisingly, most people were nice not creepy or soliciting, chatted with them, and gave directions with patience. Words like hon' and Miss or Ma'am still existed here. Most buildings were well cared for. Nacht fell asleep on a chair where sunlight filtered through vintage lace curtains, oblivious to strangers and live music.

"Looking forward to the Renaissance Faire tomorrow?" Celeste asked.

"Heck yeah. You gonna dress up?"

"I'll be a crazy cat wench," Celeste replied.

Oh, you're going as yourself, Nacht surmised.

Telly went on, "What wows me is of all the places in America, you choose small towns. You have tourists, but it's not like a packed tourist trap. It's disarming. Your Renaissance and Celtic Faires are still going strong. So many cultures don't even dream of celebrating fantasy."

"It's part historical."

"Still going to catch cats?"

"Yeah, I hope we can tame some."

"Call me if you need help. I'll drive us tomorrow," Telly

volunteered, rising. "I have another car."

"Sweet, thanks."

After their new friend left, Celeste turned to her cat. "Your instincts are better than mine. What do you think of her?"

I like her.

"Why?"

She's genuine. Even a dog or a bird could tell that. We can sniff bullcrap a mile away and I don't mean the stinky piles of turds."

Nodding in agreement, Celeste glanced at twilight sky. Twinkling lights came on outside, like lazy fireflies napping in the trees. For a retirement town, locals and visitors sure populated the streets. She tucked Nacht into her pet sling and drove to their cottage.

Celeste moved to the back porch. Solar lights cast gentle light upon pathways that wound through the yard. She saw a few retreating felines. "Well, here goes. Time to bait the traps." Not hearing Nacht grumble under his breath, Celeste opened a can of sardines and set the traps. They were good traps with quiet doors that wouldn't hurt a hapless stray. A pair of green eyes squinted out from beneath the shed, the solid gray cat.

"Ooh, you're the mama. I'm trying to help you, I swear."

The grey cat hissed. *Humans don't help us! Stay away from my kittens, you heathenistic hooman! We don't want inside!*

Celeste sounded offended. "Whoa, I'm not heathenistic."

The cat's eyes widened, then narrowed. *You speak cat? Impossible!* Her stink-eye returned, and she vanished into darkness.

Celeste sighed, returning inside. She and Nacht settled for the evening, where she updated her daily journal with photos and videos of local life and the feral cats outside.

"Mama cat sure told me off," Celeste confessed. "I've never met cats so hard to catch."

They're wild, Celeste, Nacht said, head-butting her. *I hate traps.*

Celeste petted him. "I'm sorry, but the trap's the only way on a tight schedule. It could take weeks to befriend them or," her voice saddened, "maybe never."

The kittens outside proved hungry and gullible. Celeste didn't have to wait long before Nacht jumped up and ran to the back door. *You got one! The gullible silvery guy.*

Celeste sprang to her feet and rushed outside. "Let's go see!"

Nacht stayed at a distance, his tail lashing at the noise of a scared cat banging around in the trap. It brought back memories that he didn't even tell Celeste, not yet. Memories of a scarred landscape, a pack of half wild cat friends, and a beautiful calico girlfriend, gnawed at his emotions. He watched as Celeste strode past, carrying a trap with a beach towel over it. She talked sweetly as the kitten cussed and bawled for his mom. Nacht couldn't resist. He followed. *This should be amusing.*

At a glimpse, the kitten was clearly half grown, and thus, set in his ways. Nacht snickered at the rude vocabulary of this little guy. He figured that Mama grey swore a lot.

The trapped kitten glowered up at Celeste and ranted some more. *Wait till my mom gets her claws into you! Never trust a hooman! You took our rat, didn't you? Mangy, pirating, thieves! Your mama was an ape!*

Celeste set the cage down in the guest bathroom. "You're no prince charming, either. Stay there." She walked out.

Stay there. Very funny, he growled.

Celeste returned with a bunch of cat stuff. She set up food, water, a little cat bed, a folded fluffy blanket, and a cat carrier. She turned on a night light and turned off the main, glaring, lights. Before leaving, she opened the trap.

You set him loose in there? Ha ha, Nacht teased in mock drama.

Nobody slept much that night. The kitten was either bold or frightened enough to let the world know how feisty he could be. For hours, he meowed insults and banged around in the guest bathroom.

Celeste sat up in bed, yawning. "One a.m.," she sighed,

clambering out of bed. She petted Nacht, who lay beside her. "We're lucky to get a vet appointment this week! Two more days of his racket." Celeste shuffled to her bathroom. "Kitten, I've never trapped before. We just gotta wing it." Concerned, she cracked open the guest bathroom door. "Are you okay?"

The kitten was visible in the nightlight's glow. He was half grown, a hard age to tame. Food and litter were scattered about. He glared at her before diving under the cat bed.

"You little brat, I'm gonna name you Taz the Spaz!"

Taz peeked up at her, only his silvery white face and glinting, green eyes showing. Shortly after she closed the door, he continued ranting. A weary three a.m. ticked past. Finally, the meows faded to blissful silence.

Celeste was dragging more than usual as she fixed the cats' breakfast. She almost poured her milk into the cat food and the cat food into the cereal bowl. Heating a freezer toasted waffle and a protein shake for her own breakfast, she hastened to get ready, left food and water outside for the other ferals and checked on Taz. The little guy had ignored his food and bed. He jumped behind the toilet, hissing at her.

She closed the door. "Okay, later."

*   *   *

Nacht was nursing every bit of sleep he could muster while his lady trudged about the place, grumbling. Neither of them were morning people. Nacht yawned when Celeste petted him.

"Wake up. Have you seen Taz?"

Yeah, I dreamed about him shutting up, he mumbled.

"It's no joke, I can't find him!"

How can you lose a cat in the bathroom?

"He must have slipped past me when I fed him. I was really sleepy. Help me look for him."

Nacht rolled over with a luxurious stretch. *Where's he gonna go? He's just hiding.* He ducked when the doorbell

141

rang.

"I bet that's Telly. We gotta go in a bit. Look for him, will you? Sniff him out."

Nacht walked out of the room, his tail lashing. *Oh, reduced to dog duties again.*

Celeste opened the front door and hurried their guest inside. As they talked, Nacht roamed around the place, meowing. He wasn't too surprised when Taz didn't answer, but he could smell him. Nobody in the dog carrier. Nacht hopped into the bathtub, nope. It was a strange tub, with things that looked like drains on the sides. Nacht looked behind the toilet. Next, he clawed open the cabinet door. Then he heard it, a muffled meow from under the bathtub. He pawed at a decorative plastic cover, which rattled slightly. A thump responded from the other side. Taz was smacking at him and hissing.

How'd you do that, you little moron?

You're a motley hooman lover! Taz hissed in a whisper.

Nacht trotted out to join the ladies. Maybe two women meant double the treats.

"Did you find him?" Celeste asked, her tone a mix of worry and hope.

He's okay. He insulted me and hid.

After a brief debate, the gals trusted Nacht's word, but wanted to know where this hiding spot was. So, he showed them. Grumbling in disbelief, Celeste pulled loose the jet tub's side cover. From the darkness, Taz peeked out to see who disturbed his privacy. He sat down, way back under the tub, leering at them.

Celeste straightened. "You call that okay?"

Nacht shrugged, licking himself.

Telly took a turn, lying on her belly with a flashlight, trying to coax out the little guy. Taz called them rat eating turd mongers.

Telly chuckled, shaking her head. "He'll be okay."

With some reluctance, Celeste agreed.

*   *   *

142

Celeste and Nacht headed out with Telly. They had hit it off and something about the historical, century-old buildings of Northern California lured Telly in. It could be welcoming attitudes of people, chat that felt genuine, or the relaxed non-big-city pace. Mom and Pop shops had better food than most chain restaurants. They saw people with mellow dogs in two cafes and one lumber store. Of course, Nacht, in his harness riding in Celeste's open backpack, soaked up attention.

"I like it here," Telly said. "Why'd you move to England?"

"Jobs, and I love castles." Celeste glanced at the time.

*   *   *

Taz had plenty of time to sulk while he waited in the guest bathroom. Nacht tried to comfort him, to no avail. Taz wasn't happy at all. He preferred his cubby in the shed to fluffy towels and a cat bed. The sandbox, a big bowl of water, and wet food weren't all bad, though. He mulled over the weird humans of this place:

Celeste, who had trapped him, answered his every grumble as if she knew cat language. Stranger still, he understood her. It was like magic. His mama Serena had taught him and his siblings that big folk who truly spoke to cats was only magic and fairy tales. But Celeste understood him, didn't she? Maybe this was a nightmare. He had to escape this stupid cottage.

*   *   *

The next morning, Celeste set Taz's food and treats in the trap and left the trap open. "Breakfast, yummy yum." She saw his shadowy face and glinting eyes peek at her from around the tub before he vanished into hiding again. "Fine," she sighed, rising.

After breakfast, Celeste played clips from last year's Renaissance Faire on her laptop for Nacht. "See, this is what goes on. It's people in costumes with animals, but you're cooler."

143

Nacht jumped onto the table and watched the colorful historical spectacles. He saw women dressed as wenches, men as Vikings, knights, in strange garments. Some men dressed in tin cans waving pointy things at each other. His favorite show had parrots. Nacht nosed the screen. *Holy snap, those parakeets are huge! They even talked. Bring one home. I can eat for a week.* He jumped at the sound of gunfire coming from the laptop and leapt off the table, fur hackled.

"They also have flintlock-rifles and cannons. Besides, you can't have a parrot. They bite harder than you do." Celeste stroked his soft fur. "Stay home this time? Try to comfort Taz."

Nacht rubbed against her. *I'll stay, for you.*

*   *   *

Celeste's ride drove up, and the two were off. After the gals left the cottage, Nacht walked by the bathroom wishing the door was open, but they had left Taz secured inside. He meowed, *Oh kitten, they're gone.* Nacht pawed at the door handle's lever. After a few tries, he pushed the door open. *They bought treats. I'm gonna eat them all.*

Taz retorted: *How can you be friends with her? She's a hooman!*

Nacht replied in a comforting tone: *She's my friend.*

Hoomans speaking cat is weird. Besides, my mama's waiting for me.

Nacht snuck closer to the open tub siding. *Come on, let's goof off.*

Taz shrank back and growled, fur hackling. *Go AWAY! Yeesh, brat.*

Nacht explored the whole house, finding a sunny window overlooking the backyard. He smelled cats among the scents of flowers, trees, and human things. Sure enough, a gray cat was sneaking through the landscaped yard, tail lashing upon encountering where the trap had been.

Nacht meowed at her, *Hey, you smell like a mama.*

The grey cat had a constant leer in her eyes. She looked up at Nacht and uttered a long hiss.

Nacht stood up on his hind legs, pawing at the glass. *Woo-hoo, I bet you're looking for your kid. He's in here!* Boy, could she swear.

* * *

Celeste and Telly caught all the sights the Faire, from a joust to a line for meat pies, and saw the hawks and parrot shows. A rare storyteller imitated Shakespeare with surprising accuracy, but Celeste kept thinking of the cats. She'd often mutter, "I hope Taz is okay."

Telly nudged Celeste. "Your kitties are safe. This is an interesting way to see America."

"What, local sights and helping strays? Yeah. I've gotta buy a turkey leg for Nacht."

On the way home, Telly gestured toward the thinning woods around them. "Cool towns, and the knights didn't look shabby." She parked and let Celeste out. "That was fun. We'll go out with your cat again, and it *is* beautiful here. I look forward to your stories and articles."

Celeste grabbed her bag and hopped out. "Great!"

Telly waved, driving away.

Celeste entered the cottage, and saw the bathroom door open. "Crap! Where's Taz?" After walking in circles, searching, she found Nacht in the tub, tail swishing. "Figures. You love these swag door handles." She tapped on the tub. "You still in there?" Hearing a muffled hiss, she sighed in relief. "Okay." Celeste shut Taz inside the room.

* * *

That night, around three a.m., the trap in the bathroom clanked shut. Celeste's voice piped from the bedroom, "Finally! I gotcha. You're gonna see the vet, Taz."

Nacht peeked out from under the blankets. *Then what happens to him? I'll tell you right now he's not taming any time soon. He's half grown, full of spit 'n vinegar like his mama.*

Celeste petted him before clambering out of bed. "Relax, we need mousers. The wild ones can live here. We'll make apartments in the shed and give them cat doors."

*   *   *

Taz fumed after Celeste herded him into a carrier. He whispered to Nacht, *How can you help her? How come that crazy cat lady speaks cat so good?*

Oh, now you're talking to me. He padded closer to the carrier. *Celeste is getting better at cat speech. Either she's magical, or she's from space.*

"I'm not from space," Celeste said, walking over.

But there are spaceships, Nacht reasoned.

Or magic is real, Taz growled.

Nacht flashed his teeth in a smile. *If you only knew. That'd be a story.*

 Roberta "Bert" Davis has always been a fan of sci-fi/fantasy stories, classical literature and mythology. Most of her career was in aviation maintenance in the Air Force as a crew chief, traveling worldwide, but for the last two years as a historian, retiring from the AF Reserves as a MSgt. She now works as a tech writer by day, sci-fi author by night.

She's published in anthologies from two writer's clubs, predominantly with a series of feral cat stories starring a black cat named Nacht. *Morphers and Mayhem* is her first novel, with more stories in process. A steadfast supporter of animal and wildlife rescue, Berta has four cats and cares for a small feral cat colony. She hopes to use her experience in aviation and the magic of science fiction and fantasy to tell exciting, fulfilling tales. Her goals are to expand her published works as a freelance writer/graphic designer and hopefully, an animal behaviorist.

Facebook: Roberta Davis | Facebook

https://www.facebook.com/Dragonscriber

GRAND CANYON HONEYMOON

SANDRA D. SIMMER

The car trunk lid of our Volkswagen Scirocco slammed shut with a satisfying thud. It was a sunny San Diego day in April 1984, and my new husband, Bob, and I were finally packed for our honeymoon road trip. It hadn't been easy to determine the perfect itinerary. Bob liked to be spontaneous and I liked to make plans. After lengthy negotiations, we'd come to a compromise. I planned the first half of our week-long vacation and Bob "planned" the second half. I wanted a little glamour in our honeymoon. Reservations for three days in a Las Vegas hotel, complete with a show, seemed the ideal solution. Meanwhile, Bob put our backpacks, camping tent, and other supplies into the car. He wanted to be ready to camp outdoors if we found a special location. His travel plan was open-ended with no specific destination in mind other than touring the Southwest. As we'd taken several enjoyable impromptu camping trips together, I agreed to go where the wind blew us in our sporty little Scirocco.

Located mid-strip, the budget-friendly Flamingo Hotel seemed the perfect spot for graduate students in our late twenties. We enjoyed the slot machines, buffet meals, and watermelon smashing comedian acts of 1980s Las Vegas. But after three days of noise and nightlife, the glitz and glamour wore thin.

"Where shall we go next?" I asked on the morning of our third day. "I'm ready for a change of scenery."

I hated to admit it, but my planned vacation was second-rate. The atmosphere of the Las Vegas strip wasn't awe-inspiring or even exciting. While having a comfortable bed was great, perhaps sleeping under the stars would be more romantic. It would certainly be refreshing after the cigarette smoke-filled casinos.

"Well, it isn't far to the Grand Canyon. Shall we make it our first stop?" Bob suggested. "I've always wanted to go there. Vegas was okay, but let's try something different."

Bob grew up in Ohio, and spent years learning camping skills in the Boy Scouts. His troop hiked the Smoky Mountains, and took a trip to Pike's Peak in Colorado, but missed hiking the most famous national park in the United States. Though I grew up in Southwest Colorado, I'd never seen the Grand Canyon either.

"Yes, great idea!" I agreed. "I'd like to go there, too. A few days in nature sounds wonderful." Happy with our new destination, Bob steered the Scirocco across the desert in search of adventure.

After a few hours of driving, we pulled up to the ranger's station at the south rim of the Grand Canyon around noon-time. There was still a dusting of late-spring snow on the ground and it was chilly at the 7000-foot altitude. Though the park was open, we were the only people in the vicinity. Bob began a conversation with the ranger, and asked about campsites. He also casually inquired if it was possible to hike to the bottom of the canyon. The ranger explained, to preserve the Canyon's ecosystem, they limit the number of people who visit the bottom. It's necessary to make hiking reservations as much as a year in advance. As we had no previous intension of making the hike, we weren't disappointed by his news. However, the ranger looked us over then nonchalantly mentioned, "We had a cancellation today. Are you prepared to leave right now? You can hike to the bottom on the Kaibab Trail, camp at Phantom Ranch overnight, and then hike up the Bright Angel Trail tomorrow. A park shuttle can bring you back to your car. Do you want to take the reservation?"

Bob and I stared at each other. After the disappointment of Las Vegas, here was the universe offering us our honeymoon adventure. Our futures would be filled with graduation, career advancement, buying a home, and starting a family. This was a once-in-a-lifetime chance to hike in one of Earth's most famous natural wonders, and make our dream of a memorable honeymoon come true.

"Most people who visit the park are satisfied with peering over the rim," the ranger continued. "They stop by the gift shop, and take a few photographs; pleased they've been *to* the Grand Canyon. But few people have been *in* the Grand Canyon. Even fewer have hiked to the bottom. You'll be part of an elite group of sightseers."

"Let's do it," Bob said. "All the stuff we need is in the car. We can leave in 30 minutes."

Being the cautious one of the pair, I asked the ranger, "How far down is it to the bottom, and how long will it take to get there?"

The ranger seemed eager to help. "It's about six miles down the Kaibab trail. It should take you about four to five hours to reach the bottom. You walk downhill on switchbacks most of the way and can make pretty good time. If you leave now, you'll reach the ranch well before dark."

"Can we eat dinner at Phantom Ranch?"

"No, you need reservations for meals, too. All the food is hauled in by mules. They don't have food to spare. You'll need to pack your own food down, and bring any trash back up."

This was beginning to sound a little more difficult than I expected. "Why do we come up a different trail?" I asked. "Isn't it the same distance back up?"

"Well, no, actually it's a little farther that route, but it's an easier hike out. It's about nine miles back up on Bright Angel, but the first five miles to the plateau aren't bad. Then you only have four miles of steep trails to climb at the end. You should be fine after a night's rest."

That information did not make me feel more confident, but Bob was still enthusiastic to give it a try.

"Come on! We can do it. It's all downhill today, and we can take our time tomorrow. It'll be fun and a great story to tell our grandkids!" he said with a wink.

I got caught up in the idea of doing something extraordinary. The posters scattered around the ranger's station boasted of the Grand Canyon as one of the seven natural wonders of the world. The meandering Colorado River had worn away layers of Earth's geologic history over millions of years. The canyon is miles wide and a mile deep. The sides are cut so irregularly at the deepest points you can't see the canyon floor from the top. We couldn't fully appreciate the wonder of the magnificent "beast" without venturing into its belly.

"Okay," I said, "I'll give it a try. We can come back up if it seems too hard, right?"

"Sure you can," said the ranger. "Just don't be on the trail when it gets dark. There's a marker on the trail at the halfway point. If you go past it, you'll have to hike to the bottom."

Bob and I jumped into action. We pulled our camping items out of the car and laid them on the ground. It was immediately clear we couldn't carry everything. The tent, portable stove, and cookware went back into the trunk. Bob imagined we could find some kind of shelter at the ranch. We sorted the food to remove anything that required cooking. The few remaining supplies included a can of spam, beef jerky, peanut butter cracker snacks, two apples, and a large bag of trail mix. We had intended to buy fresh food items before setting up a campsite.

Though it was cold on top of the canyon, the ranger said it was actually several degrees warmer at the bottom. He suggested we dress in layers. We pulled on jackets over sweaters and added waterproof ponchos on top. Though we didn't have hiking boots, our running shoes had cushioned inserts and plenty of tread on the bottom. The food, personal items, and bottled water filled our backpacks. Bob added sleeping bags and a lightweight ground pad to his load. With our layered outerwear and burgeoning backpacks, we looked like a couple of desert tortoises carrying our homes on our backs.

The ranger stamped a ticket and tied it to Bob's pack. He said another ranger at the bottom would ask to see our permit. Then he waved us out the door. We walked briskly to the head of the trail to start our big adventure.

While I was young and fairly fit, I wasn't an athlete. I'd

been on one backpacking expedition as a college student, and a few tent camping trips. My biggest physical accomplishment to date was a twelve-mile bike ride on a flat desert highway near Yuma, Arizona. I could jog a couple of miles, but that was about it. Bob was a little more fit than me, but the last few years we'd been working and going to graduate school. Our imagined level of fitness didn't match the reality of the physical exertion needed for the mission we undertook. However, the excitement of the moment overcame any sensible objections.

The trail at the top was wide enough for us to walk side by side and enjoy the scenery. The air felt cold at first, and I was glad for my warm layers of clothing. As the trail made sharp turns back and forth along the ridge, it was tempting to take a shortcut to the level below. However, the elevation drop between the switchbacks was too steep. Not wanting to risk a sprained ankle, we continued to slowly weave our way down the slope.

It felt like we had hiked for a long time, and there was still no sign of the river. The canyon was stair-stepped by erosion, and the view down was blocked by plateaus. As we strode along the pathway, red colored earth rose up in dust clouds to cover our tennis shoes in a ruddy powder. The farther down we went the higher the rock formations rose to tower above us. The raw beauty of the colorful rocks and the pungent sage brush began to permeate our senses. No other hikers were on the trail, and the wildlife kept hidden in the desolate environment. Only the occasional bird call could be heard as the shadow of a hawk passed overhead. The solitary setting seemed to reject conversation. After a few giddy comments about our good fortune, Bob and I fell into a companionable silence. The magnificence of the setting was overwhelming, and I became aware of our insignificance in this foreign place. The eons of time were being revealed with each new level of descent. It felt as if we could be hiking on the distant red planet Mars. Perhaps we were walking through similar particles of dust. It was awe inspiring, humbling, and peaceful all at once.

At the half- way-point trail marker, we stopped to drink

water and eat the apples. "How are you feeling?" asked Bob. "We still can't see the river from here. Do you want to keep going?"

I turned to look back up the trail. It appeared much steeper than when we started. It wouldn't be an easy hike back to the car, and it was already late afternoon.

"I'm okay," I said. "I needed a break. I'm getting tired of carrying this pack, but I'd rather keep hiking downhill. We've come this far. Let's go all the way to the bottom." I was determined to reach our goal.

"All right," agreed Bob, "I'm glad you want to keep going. It's amazing being the only two people out here. Are you feeling the vibrations coming off the rocks?"

"That's just your feet throbbing," I teased. But I too felt the mystical power of the setting. It was too majestic to put into words. I gave Bob a hug and started back down the trail in front of him this time.

The wind had started to blow across the trail. It was a warm desert sirocco-like wind, warmed from the canyon floor, and felt pleasant at first. We kept zigzagging down the trail until, around a bend; the river appeared far below us. "Hooray!" we shouted, as we danced with excitement. Clouds of red dust rose to surround us. I wanted a picture of our first glimpse of the river. To include it in the camera shot, I had Bob step closer to the edge. At that very moment, the wind blew a strong blast of air down the trail. It filled up Bob's poncho like a balloon, and drove him to the edge of the ravine. His heavy pack threw him off balance, and he stumbled towards the edge.

"Bob," I gasped. I fumbled to grab his arm. "Be careful!" Fortunately, the wind subsided as quickly as it appeared, and he was able to scramble back onto firm ground. We hugged in a tight embrace and thanked our Higher Power for protective intervention. Though the afternoon sun was creating a colorful rainbow across the Canyon walls, the remote setting had lost some of its charm. The reality of our immense undertaking sobered our mood, and we directed our remaining energy towards safely reaching Phantom Ranch before dark.

Two hours later we slowly walked into the ranch; a few buildings set upon open ground at a bend in the river. I had never been so tired and hungry in my life. Hiking expended a lot of energy, and the snack food hadn't kept me satisfied. Bob wanted to save the trail mix for the next day, so I'd been gnawing on beef jerky for the last hour. After the on-site ranger reviewed our permit, we headed to the dining hall to check on leftovers. A nice lady located one tuna sandwich she sold us for ten dollars, but had nothing more to offer. We shared the sandwich and our single can of Spam. It felt like we had eaten a feast.

Unreserved sleeping accommodations were non-existent. There were no barns or lean-tos to offer shelter. A dilapidated picnic table provided a roof over our heads for the night. We spread out the thin foam ground pad and placed our sleeping bags on top. They were zipped together, not because it was our honeymoon, but to help us stay warm. Too exhausted to notice the hard surface, we cuddled together and fell into a fitful sleep.

The next day my eyelids popped open with the first ray of sunlight, but I couldn't move anything else with ease. Every muscle in my body ached. My legs were as rigid as the legs on the picnic table. I could hardly get off the ground. Bob was equally stiff and sore. I panicked when I thought about hiking up the canyon wall.

"Do they have helicopters to rescue people?" I cried. "Can they put me on one of those mules? You're going to have to leave me here to die. I can't do it!"

"Don't worry," Bob cheerfully announced, "we'll use our front leg muscles to climb up the canyon wall. We used our back leg muscles going downhill. You'll be fine."

His comments only fueled my frustration until I realized there really wasn't an alternative exit. I had to climb out. There was no point in crying over sore muscles.

By the time I ate my trail mix breakfast, my body had loosened up a bit. The morning hike up a gradual slope wasn't difficult, and we arrived at a mountain meadow before noon. There were restrooms and fresh water at the trail break. I felt refreshed and ready to continue, until I saw the trail ahead. My heart began to pound. The last four-mile section went straight up the side of a granite mountain.

Bob found two sturdy fallen tree branches that he trimmed into walking sticks with his Boy Scout knife. "Here, hon," he said, "you're doing great. We can use these to help pull ourselves up the trail. Just concentrate on one step at a time."

I nodded, too discouraged to speak, and followed his lead. To avoid looking down, I focused on the back of his neck peeking out above his jacket collar. His neck was colored a dark red by the sun and the ruddy canyon soil. To distract myself from pain and hunger, I visualized taking a hot shower and eating a steak dinner. I kept putting one foot in front of the other, pulling myself along with the help of the makeshift walking stick. Other, more experienced, hikers on the trail gave us a cheerful "hello", as they hurried past.

The Bright Angel trail was a whole different experience. It was carved into the granite side of a cliff and was very narrow. Pieces of rock scattered along the trail surface made the footing precarious. At one point a line of pack mules came down the trail while we were climbing up. Bob and I flattened our backs to the granite wall and let the animals pass on the cliff side. I changed my mind about riding a mule on such a harrowing trail. Using my own strength to pull myself up the mountain seemed the wisest tactic.

I reflected on how Bob and I'd tested our physical and mental stamina. We'd discovered we could survive unexpected challenges together. Determination and flexibility were key ingredients of our success. We experienced, plan or not, that positive outcomes aren't guaranteed. We learned to admire and respect nature at the same time. Our honeymoon trip was special in so many ways.

When we finally reached the trailhead, it ended at the park's gift shop. Tourists were milling around marveling at the hikers who'd conquered the beast. Bob and I smiled at their comments of congratulations, but didn't stop to discuss our journey. Instead, we painfully lumbered tortoise-like across the parking lot towards the shuttlebus stop. We had the rest of our lives to retell our honeymoon adventure. First, we needed to find the nearest luxury hotel.

Sandra D. Simmer comes from a family of artisans that nurtured her creative spirit. She maintained her interest in the arts while raising a family and pursuing a career in non-profit management. Sandra enjoys traveling and has experienced many interesting travel adventures.

Recently retired to the San Francisco Bay Area, Sandra has followed her love of the written word to write about her colorful life: both real and imagined. She joined several writing groups and credits her mentor friends with expanding her writing skills. Sandra also thanks her children, Erin and Bryce, for their encouragement to take chances with her new writing career.

Sandra is a newly published author with stories in the NCPA's anthologies *Destination: the World Volumes I & II, All Holidays 2020 and All Holidays Vol 2.* She is currently writing her first novel.

Sandra can be found on LinkedIn and contacted at sandpiper99@hotmail.com.

MONUMENTS
SCOTT CHARLES

The nights when he was especially lonely and needed to feel a connection with life, Greg Bishop would go to a certain office building in Detroit.

He would talk and drink coffee with Jerry, the muscular, red-haired maintenance foreman. The twelve midnight-to-eight A.M. shift was dull, and Jerry welcomed a break in the routine.

At some point the conversation would work its way to a conclusion and Bishop would go up to the roof with his binoculars and lift his spirit by watching the city. Jerry had no particular interest in the roof, aside from making sure it was well kept and secure, so Bishop would stand there alone in the night air watching the city put itself to sleep.

Early one morning the investor, who had purchased Bishop's construction company, called him and invited him to attend a builders' convention at Cobo Hall. Several prominent bankers and stockholders would be in attendance, and the investor had asked Bishop to come along and explain the finer points of interpreting new trends, cost analysis, and general contracting. The hall was full of giant dump trucks, tractors, diggers, trenchers, dirt conveyors, insulation and irrigation systems.

Bishop's personality was still powerful, and the exuberance and eloquence with which he recalled his former professional insights had impressed everyone.

After the cocktail party he took a cab home, walked through the front door feeling twenty years younger, and almost called his wife's name. He wanted to talk to someone, share the events of the day and relax.

But there was no one to hear him. His wife had died years ago and his children were long grown and out of the house.

He went to the bedroom and took the family albums out of the bottom dresser drawer. He turned the pages slowly, touching each photograph gently. Dark haired Cathy, his wife, and his two daughters, Jennifer and Emily.

"They don't need me anymore," he said to the empty house. He put the album away, took his binoculars out of the closet and went to see Jerry.

Jerry had been in the supply room, a small six-by-eight space that had equipment hanging on every sea-green cement wall, when he heard Joe, the security guard, unlock one of the glass doors. Jerry stepped out and around the corner just as Bishop smothered a cigarette in a sand filled ashtray.

"Hi there," Bishop said to Joe, extending his hand. "I'm Greg Bishop."

Joe shook Bishop's hand and simply said, "Joe."

"Hey, Greg," said Jerry. "C'mon in and have a cup of coffee. I made it extra strong, on account a' the weather."

"Don't mind if I do," Bishop replied.

The two men walked towards Jerry's tiny office space. Joe went back to his station in the lobby.

Bishop hung his coat on a hook, setting his hickory walking stick by the door, "So how's the wife and kids, Jerry? Keepin' ya busy, I bet."

Jerry nodded and gave Bishop a mug of warm coffee. "Yep. Never a dull moment. Chasing one of 'em while I'm holding the other. The wife says I'll make a good father in spite of myself."

"I know what you mean, Jerry. Just wait 'till they discover whatever's next. By the way – that new guy, Joe? Kind of a somber sort, isn't he?"

"Yeah, well, he's a good guy," Jerry replied. "I think he's just lonely. Maybe a little depressed. His wife died last year."

"I see," Bishop said, and left it at that.

"So, let's see what we have here," Jerry said, and reached into the top drawer of a beat-up old desk and brought out a deck of cards. With a gleam in his eye, he began shuffling. Bishop chuckled and matched him twinkle for gleam.

"What?" Bishop asked with mock incredulity, "last time wasn't enough? I guess you don't know when you're beat."

"We'll just see about that," Jerry replied, presenting the deck to him, offering a cut. "The name of the game, sir, is Tonk."

"Quarter if you go down, fifty cents for a Tonk, dollar if you burn?" asked Bishop.

"Chickenfeed!" replied Jerry. "Fifty cents if you go down with ten or less, a buck for a Tonk, and two bucks if you burn. Can you handle it?"

Bishop slapped his knee with genuine delight. "I love it! Deal 'em!"

After an hour Jerry had managed to win ten dollars and Bishop decided to quit with the younger man in the plus column.

"You gonna come up to the roof with me?" he asked, slipping on his coat and gloves.

"No "Jerry replied, "I want to go up to eight and nine, I got a crew up there, want to see if they're working."

Heading for the elevator, they passed by Joe, who overheard them and said, "Yeah, the lobby floor could use some care too."

The lobby tile, white geometric on a shale-grey background, wasn't dirty but definitely needed to be stripped and waxed.

"I'll take care of it, Joe," replied Jerry.

"And Molly's been asking about the gift shop too. The glass," Joe said pointing across the lobby, "She's been leaving notes for me every day for a week."

The elevator came down and the doors opened. "I already talked to Molly, Joe. No need to worry about it."

Bishop looked down at his shoes and stifled a laugh. "Nice meeting you, Joe," he said. Joe stared at them but said nothing.

For a moment the two men were weightless as the elevator halted at the eighth floor. The doors opened and Jerry stepped out. "I'll see you later, Greg. If not later tonight, then next time around."

He nodded, the door closed, and Bishop took the elevator up to the twentieth floor and climbed the single flight of stairs to the roof.

The wind was an icy demon, whipping Bishop's sparse gray hair across his forehead and into his eyes. He tightened the collar of his corduroy overcoat, took out his knit stocking cap, the green one his granddaughter had made for him as a birthday present, and pulled it down over his ears.

Bishop walked to the north wall, hunched slightly to keep the wind from his face. The tar paper and pea gravel combination that covered the roof made a slightly crunchy sound as he walked past pipes with bright red valves, metal duct work dulled gray by the sun, wind, and rain, the roof vents and black exhaust pipes rising up. He went to the northwest corner, took the binoculars out of their leather case, leaned into the corner angle and put his elbows on top of the block wall.

The traffic on Highway 75 was heavy. The John Lodge, Jefferson and 94 exits were receiving a steady stream of cars. Bishop saw them as lights cutting through the darkness at high speeds, catching only glimpses of the automobiles that carried them along.

In the distance he could see factories, warehouses, and residential sections. In one place 75 dipped below ground level with three tiers of curving freeway above it. In other places there were overpasses and a few pedestrian bridges enclosed in plexiglass, or wire mesh.

A police car turned on its blue and red lights, rocketed by the general traffic, and raced down an exit.

Bishop coughed. His nose was red, his forehead and cheeks stinging from the cold wind.

He walked along the east wall, watching dim shadow people move along the street below, until he came to the southeast corner. He looked out across the water.

The Detroit River was dark and wide. A few cargo ships and tankers moved leisurely beneath the Ambassador Bridge, portholes lit.

Against the cloudy sky, moonlight filtered through and gave the heavens a white radiance. Across the river, Windsor was outlined against the horizon.

"Beautiful," he whispered. The night sky answered him with twinkling stars.

Bishop couldn't stand the chill any longer. Shivering, he put the binoculars away and took the elevator back down to the lobby. Jerry was in the supply room looking over a clipboard that had some order forms attached.

Making his way towards the lobby door, Bishop stopped, paused a moment and stuck his head in the supply room. "So, when are we going to shoot some pool?" he asked.

Jerry grinned. "Saturday over at the T-Bird?"

"We'll see you on Saturday," Bishop replied.

As he walked out the lobby door, he told Joe "Nice meeting you", but Joe didn't reply so Bishop left it at that and walked out to the sidewalk.

Tapping his cane gently as he went along, he regarded the people he passed with varying degrees of interest. He decided to take an unusual route and avoid the nightly crowds. After a while the streets were almost deserted with only the occasional couple holding hands, or someone walking their dog.

When he came to a vaguely familiar row of small shops, he noted they were all closed except for the last one, a small corner bar, whose flickering neon sign said Dell's. He thought perhaps he should stop in and have a beer, but decided against it. The place looked a bit too rough that evening.

Making his way to an intersection, Bishop got a taxi and had the driver drop him off a few blocks from home.

The rest of the walk to Phillips Street was uneventful. The branches of the elms and maples he passed were bare. Fallen leaves blew past his legs. There was a cold breeze, so he raised the collar of his jacket. Occasionally a cat ran across the street or a branch creaked in the wind.

Bishop came to his block. The streets were empty. The streetlights, little moons, cast their light in spots, leaving shadows everywhere else. There, up ahead, was his house.

He let his cane rattle across the points of his picket fence. The moonlight made them look silver.

He walked up the flagstone path to his screened in porch, unlocked the door and sat down on the swing.

Again, thinking about his latest nightmare, the one where he was dying, slowly, one breath at a time, he knew in that dream that when he took his last breath everything he knew, or felt, all the learned wisdom and whatever was left of his ambition to do something more – it would all be gone. Every time he had that dream, he woke up struggling for breath.

Bishop clenched his hand over his heart and made a tight fist. "I can feel it! All of it. Right here! I can feel it. In my loins. I can feel it my blood! And for what? I'll die and it won't matter. Gone! All of it."

Standing up, flushed with anger, he raised his cane at the swing. He stopped in mid-swing, breathing hard, his face red and clammy. He took a deep breath, forced himself to relax, closed the screen door gently, locked it, then went in the front door. He went straight to his bedroom and went to bed.

He slept poorly and woke up knowing he had been dreaming, but thankful he couldn't remember any of it. He didn't feel quite right but assumed it was lack of sleep.

Bishop made breakfast and had a cup of coffee. But something was wrong. The chill of the night breeze was still in his chest. His lungs tickled him into fits of coughing until he was spitting out yellow phlegm speckled with blood.

Phoning his doctor, he misdialed twice before settling himself and got the right number. He called Doctor Allyn who told him to get over to Saint John's. Not wanting to drive himself, he called his daughter.

They gave him a private room with a television, told him no smoking. The food was good and the staff was pleasant and respectful. But no matter how good the care was, Bishop didn't like being in the hospital. He didn't like lying around and he didn't like the medicinal smell.

"How's your golf game, Max?" he said as Dr. Allyn came into the room, checked the chart, and sat down next to the bed.

"Not much better. Can't break eighty," replied Allyn. "The tests say pneumonia, Greg." Allyn's dark eyes were steady, his voice calm but stern.

"Well, that's what I like about you, Max. Straight to the point," replied Bishop. "But I knew that when I came in here yesterday. What else?"

"Have you had any chest pains lately?" Dr. Allyn asked.

The two men sat there for a moment. Bishop finally nodded.

"We're going to run some tests. My guess is you have some blockage."

"And?"

"If it were just pneumonia, it wouldn't be a big deal. But the heart problem changes the game. You're a tough guy, Greg, I get that, but you're over seventy and you have a family history of heart trouble. This could get complicated."

"OK. Understood," Bishop replied.

Dr. Allyn looked at the chart one more time. "I'll be back around at the end of the day." Then he got up and left the room, closing the door gently.

"Damn," Bishop said to nobody.

Jerry got a call on the fourth day of Bishop's stay at the hospital, and was just getting his pool cue out of the closet when the phone rang. He had intended to get the old cue out just to see how it felt and then go to bed. He answered the phone on the fifth ring.

"Mister Hall," said a women's voice.

"Yes?" Jerry replied.

"This is Jennifer Bishop. Greg's daughter."

"Oh yeah, hi. What can I do for you?"

"Dad's in the hospital. He'd like to see you."

"Oh? What happened?"

"He's got pneumonia. There's also something wrong with his heart. Plus, he's having a reaction to the antibiotics they're using for the pneumonia. I think it would cheer him up if you went to visit."

"All right. I'll get dressed and stop by. Just give me an hour or so."

Jerry arrived at Saint John's a little after 8:30 pm. Jennifer was in the lobby with Emily, talking to Dr. Allyn. Jennifer wasn't smiling, and Emily was wiping away tears.

Jerry hugged Jennifer, then Emily. Jennifer introduced Jerry to Dr. Allyn.

"I'm going up to the room. You can come on up with me," he said to Jerry.

In the elevator Jerry said, "From the way Jennifer and Emily looked, they don't think he's going to come through."

"He might, if he doesn't get any worse. He's seventy-five next year. Sometimes it's not one big thing, it's years of little things."

"But I was just with him a few days ago. He looked great."

"I know. He doesn't look or act his age, but there are so many different factors at play as people get older—"

"He's the best looking seventy-five I ever saw."

"I agree. He is. We'll do what we can. He's been asking for you. Hopefully it will cheer him up a bit."

Dr. Allyn paused before he opened the door to Bishop's room. "He wanted to talk to you alone. That's why his daughters are waiting in the lobby. He might be a bit drowsy, maybe even a bit disoriented. Ring for the call nurse if you need anything."

Bishop didn't look well. He had an ashen color and his palm was clammy when Jerry and he shook hands.

"So how are you, buddy?" Jerry said.

"Good morning, Jerry. Truth be told I feel lousy. But don't worry about that. I'm glad you stopped by. I want to talk to you."

"OK, Greg, whatever you say."

Bishop laughed. "You don't need to worry about bedside manner. It's just us, right?"

Jerry smiled. He was biting his lower lip, and wiped away a tear, but was smiling.

"OK, that's better," said Bishop.

The two men made small talk for a while, both of them

165

trying to come to grips with the situation. After a bit they ran out of small talk.

Bishop sighed. "When I was your age, I acted as if I was going to live forever," he said.

Jerry just nodded and waited.

"So, listen up. Maybe I'll get up and walk out of here. And maybe I don't. I may never see you again. And if that's how it turns out, I want to make sure I leave something behind. I had a life, Jerry. I was here, I did things and I felt things. A whole lifetime of feelings. So, it all comes down to one thing. I can't face death unless I'm sure that I do something special for someone, one last time. I want one more person to feel something special because of me. And I want them to pass it on to the next person. Then I can face death."

"I swear to God, Greg, there's one thing you'll never be and that's forgotten. Your kids, grandkids—"

"Yeah, I know. I get that. If I make it out of here, we'll have a beer. Shoot some pool. But in case I don't, there are a few things I want you to have – my tools mostly. Stuff like that, but the most important thing is –"

There was a rapping on the door. Dr. Allyn stepped in, glanced at Bishop then at Jerry.

"We're getting ready to transfer you to another room, Greg. And we want to do another round of tests," Dr. Allyn said.

"OK, Max. Look, Jerry, thanks for stopping by. And thanks for being my friend."

Jerry took Bishop's hand, gripped it firmly, and said, "I'll stop by later, Greg."

Jerry nodded to Dr. Allyn, walked out of the room, went to the nearest bathroom, started to cry and put some cold water on his face. He fought off the nausea and took a few moments to compose himself.

As Jerry walked out of the bathroom, Dr. Allyn was coming towards him. "Just so you know," Dr Allyn said, "it makes it easier on them if they know the people they love are going to be OK. Makes it easier on us, too."

"OK. I'll stop by tomorrow," replied Jerry. Dr. Allyn

nodded and moved on to his next patient. Jerry watched him walk away.

Jerry took a deep breath, got a quick sip of water at the drinking fountain, went back home, watched TV without really watching it, ate a small dinner without really tasting it, and went to work.

The next day Jennifer called and told him that her father's heart had stopped during the night and the staff had been unable to revive him. She said this in a matter-of-fact tone, but Jerry knew that her outward resignation masked her grief.

Greg Bishop's funeral was well attended. Jerry didn't really know anyone so he didn't linger. After the ceremony he said his condolences to Bishop's daughters and left.

A few days later there was a package waiting for him when he got to work. Inside the package was Greg Bishop's obituary, a note, a card, and a pair of binoculars.

The letter said "Jerry: I want you to have these. Take care," and was signed in Bishop's careful handwriting. The card said "Jerry: please keep in touch," and was signed "Jennifer". The handwriting was almost identical.

"Like father like daughter," he said to himself.

Joe stepped into the office to fill out his time card as Jerry was looking at the binoculars.

"I never understood exactly what he was looking at. Up on the roof I mean," Jerry said.

"Let's go see," said Joe.

The two men went to the service elevator and then to the roof. The moon was bright, and the city-scape was well lit. The clouds were moving fast in a patchwork formation. Rays of moonlight filtered through.

They made their way to the south wall. Jerry put the binoculars to his eyes and looked out across the dark waters at Windsor. A few ships drifted by, portholes glowing.

He shifted a bit and looked out across the city. Spires of concrete and steel and glass, lit up from the inside, provided a contrast to the dark blue sky. He felt the wind on his face and could see cars and people moving. A horn here and there, a siren off in the distance.

He could see life and movement, could almost feel the living vibration of it. Looking down, around, across and up, he understood. He knew what Bishop had seen.

He thought he heard someone whispering, "thank you."

"Can you see it? It's beautiful, isn't it? All that life," said Joe.

Jerry nodded "yes." He fought back tears.

Joe took out his thermos and poured them both a cup of coffee.

"You want to talk about it?" Joe asked.

"Yeah," replied Jerry.

The two men took a moment to look up at the sky. They shared the binoculars and coffee and slowly, one step at a time, began to see the world from a different perspective.

Scott Charles was born in the Midwest and relocated to Sacramento, California in the 1980s where he lives a happy life with his wife and dog.

He has released a novel, *The Illustrated Hen,* which is available on Amazon.com. *The Illustrated Hen* received a Cover Award during the 2020 NCPA Book Awards competition. Scott also has stories in several NCPA anthologies, and won the Risk Takers' Award for his story *The Ornaments*, in NCPA's *All Holidays 2020* anthology.

Scott is also the author of several plays, including *Dinners with Augie.* You can see some of his other works on his website at www.libernetics.com.

GALAPAGOS ISLANDS TREASURE HUNT

RONALD JAVOR

U nder a bright blue cloudless sky, our large, sleek tour boat left the dock on Baltra Island carrying its crew and sixteen new friends who would spend the next five nights and days cruising through Ecuador's Galapagos Islands. We already had spent eight eye-opening days together exploring Machu Pichu, the famous Incan royal estate and religious site, other parts of Peru, and mainland Ecuador. This voyage, however, the last part of our tour, was the ultimate adventure and education trip most of us had signed up for.

The night before we raised anchor, the group heard a colorful description of our impending trip from a new local tour guide, Juan Fernando. He told us we would be visiting three to four islands for walking and close-up visits to see the birds, iguanas, seals and other animals on those islands. We also would have opportunities most days for snorkeling or rafting to see fish and other animals living in their home waters.

Juan asked us to go around the room to say a little about ourselves so he would know us better. We should include why we were taking this trip and something funny or not already known to the others. Our group consisted of four couples, six single travelers like me, and a mother with her 14-year-old son, Timmy. While the descriptions of the others represented a cross-section of our society—teachers, a retired postal worker, a radio broadcaster, and a couple of retired science professionals—we heard Timmy's story for the first time. He had been diagnosed with a life-threatening illness, and during treatment his mother promised him a trip anywhere he wanted to go when he recovered. He described himself as a "science nerd" and told her that seeing the Galapagos Islands and the unique animal residents there would be his dream trip.

The next morning the boat set out after breakfast, Juan sat the group down for what he called "the lecture" and gave the history of the Islands from several viewpoints. First, he told us about the geological history, focusing on its volcanic origins and continued isolation from the South American continent. Then he reviewed the human history: its early discovery, the visit by Charles Darwin, the later abuse by visiting humans ranging from pirates to poachers, and the current efforts to preserve and revitalize its native animals and plant life. Finally, he handed out pictures, showing us the diversity of plant, animal, bird, reptile, and mammal life that abounded there, many of which were found nowhere else in the world.

After a break, Juan resumed the discussion and said there were only three rules, but violating any of them could result in a visitor being banned back to the boat for the duration of the trip and possible criminal charges when we returned to the mainland. One was that we had to stay on prepared trails unless he allowed a short walk to see a special sight. This helped preserve the habitats. The second was that we were not to touch or harm any animals or plants. And the final rule was that we could not pick up and take home anything we found there.

He finished our meeting by saying that within those constraints, he was sponsoring a treasure hunt for us and the winner would get a special Galapagos Tortoise t-shirt. Unlike other treasure hunts, we could not pick up and show our treasures. Instead, he would hand out several disposable cameras, one for use underwater and we would take pictures of the "treasures" we identified. At the end of the cruise, the pictures would be developed and printed immediately, and he and the boat's captain would select "the treasure": the picture that most reflected the essence of the Galapagos Islands, and our trip there.

As we consumed an early lunch—yes, we ate often and

well—the boat docked at our first island, Santa Cruz (sometimes called "Indefatigable") Island. Under a hot sun, we hiked for several miles and saw plodding giant land tortoises and numerous speckled land iguanas skittering about. Juan pointed out less obvious sights like a soaring enormous albatross, various small birds and their nests, and indications near the trail of small native mice. We hiked up and down scrub bush trails and walked on clean white beaches where we soaked our feet in the warm Pacific waters. Late that afternoon, as we gathered back on the boat for our pre-dinner appetizers and drinks, we all shared our awe at the great animal diversity and beauty of the island, but each person also said they'd seen nothing so unusual as to be the ultimate "treasure" for the prize.

The next day we awakened and found ourselves moored at Santiago Island. "Bring your bathing suits," Juan warned us as we prepared to leave the ship and he handed out the cameras again. We walked to an isolated bay and saw small groups of brown Galapagos hawks with their four-foot wing spans circling overhead, screeching at us, and tiny Darwin's finches and other shore birds flitting and chirping around us. We passed by lava fields and eventually arrived at a sheltered bay.

On the beach by the bay, we saw dozens of sunning light brown seals with their darker young pups sprawled out sleeping on the sand and watched and listened to enormous dark brown sea lions rolling around and barking at each other from a colony not far away. We also spotted marine iguanas going in and out of the water; these lizard-like reptiles can grow up to four feet long including their tails. They have spikes along their backs, and were described by Charles Darwin as "disgusting" and "clumsy." Juan also led us to a series of isolated tidal pools filled with small fish, crabs, shells, and sea plants displaying the full arc of a bright rainbow.

Several of us then stripped to our bathing suits, borrowed snorkels, and went into the ocean. "Don't try to pet anything" was the last we heard from Juan. The ocean water was crystal clear. As we swam along, various types of fish swarmed around us and I came almost nose-to-nose with a curious seal who suddenly appeared from nowhere. The look on its face made me wish I had the underwater camera! When I surfaced and looked back, Timmy was not swimming, but was walking around near the sea lions, taking pictures of several of them. Unfortunately, after an hour and despite still wanting to see more of the color and animal activity around us, it was time to walk back to the boat and leave this island.

Just before sunset we pulled into a bay at Española Island as two other ships left. This popular island has so much to offer that we were going to stay there for most of two days. For those who wanted to, there was a 5:00 a.m. wake-up call with a light breakfast. We boarded rafts with scuba gear and left "to see the fish come home in the morning." I had a camera for this trip and my pictures of several massive schools of fish approaching the reefs were amazing, at least to me.

Later in the morning all of us went on a "bird tour" and saw some of the most famous Galapagos birds: blue-footed boobies, masked boobies, swallow-tailed gulls, mockingbirds and doves, and other unique avian species. Some were near their nests and others fearlessly strutted near us, pecked at the ground for food or merely roosted on vegetation, singing to us. There is good reason why the blue-footed booby is such a Galapagos icon: its feet truly are bright teal blue, it has a duck-like bill, and it is about three feet long with a five-foot wingspan. All the cameras were clicking at these exotic creatures during this excursion.

The second day on Española was split: in the morning we took a long hike to visit the indigenous land animals, especially a humongous sea lion colony with its unforgettable animal sizes, noises, and particularly rancid smells. Juan told us that you distinguish a sea lion from a seal because only sea lions have external ears. We also were treated to a breeding season surprise: the marine iguanas turn red during breeding time and become far more active and aggressive than the local lava lizards and other iguanas.

At another part of the island is a protected area set aside for the famous Española great tortoises, an endangered species. As I watched Timmy, who was carrying a camera again, he took a couple of pictures of these resting animals but I noticed he also was watching the rest of us as well as the animals, almost as if he were checking to see what we were taking pictures of. I'm sure he badly wanted to win the treasure hunt prize.

Depending on individual preferences, the afternoon was spent either on our rafts exploring cliffs and sea caverns and the birds and sea life that lived on or in them, snorkeling just offshore, or merely relaxing on the beach. Timmy and I were on the same raft, and he was entranced by the giant albatross that fell from the high cliffs in order to start their flights for food; he took several pictures of them sitting and then jumping down to fly away. I donned my snorkel and mask again, and went underwater, seeing and taking pictures of large rays, small sharks, and other varied and colorful species of fish hiding in and near the cavern openings.

After dinner, Juan reviewed the next day's itinerary then said he wanted to tell us some more important information. "You've all been impressed by the types of animals and sea life you've seen, and you need to understand something else. The animals you are seeing are survivors, not just inhabitants. Relatives of some of the animals you've seen have become extinct, such as a bird, the San Cristobal vermilion flycatcher, the Galapagos giant rat, the Indefatigable Galapagos Mouse, and Darwin's Mouse. Most of these extinctions are due to human activity which is why we have the rules I told you about and why people like me work here to protect this environment.

"Other animals still living in the Galapagos Islands are threatened by extinction for many of the same reasons. These include the blue-footed boobies whose population has been reduced by two-thirds since the 1960s, the Galapagos hawk and fur seal, and the Galapagos penguin and petrel, to name a few. You've probably heard about Lonesome George, the last Pinta Island Giant Tortoise who has lived alone for over 20 years at our Conservation Center while his caretakers have sought a mate. Keep these problems in mind as you watch the animals you see and think about the reasons for the rules I mentioned the first night as well as why we try to teach you to appreciate this unique environment."

Our last stop on the final morning of the cruise was Floreana Island. It has two interesting characteristics. One is that on a walk inland we came to a "Post Office barrel" where tourists can leave addressed unstamped postcards, to be delivered when picked up by Island nature workers; whalers used to leave notices here in the 18th century to send news home to be picked up by homeward bound ships. The other is that this island is actually an underwater volcano crater and the sea life within the crater and along the protected coral is more exotic than anywhere else

This time I was able to persuade Timmy to come into the water with me, although he wore only a mask and wouldn't try the snorkel. His excitement was evident as we saw, came near to, and photographed a wide variety of sea life including stingrays, reef sharks, and even sea turtles while foraging for food, swimming near us. Other sea life just congregated and hid in the surrounding coral. At his request, I used the last couple of shots in the camera to take pictures of him there with the sea life so he'd have something to show his family and friends back home.

For our last dinner on the boat—as well as the entire tour—we ate pescado de la casa (fresh fish home-style), papas (there are over 4,000 species of potatoes grown in Peru and Ecuador and we had a dozen of them that night in our grilled potatoes), vegetales salteados (fresh sautéed vegetables), and torta de duraznos (fresh peach pie) or pastel de chocolate (chocolate cake). After dinner Juan collected the cameras and solemnly announced that none of us would be arrested upon landing since we had followed all the rules. Later the crew performed a song-and-dance skit written to imitate each of us in some humorous way and we celebrated our new friendships as the ship cruised back to our final port.

The next morning, as we ate a late breakfast, Juan came back with a sheaf of 8x10-inch photographs, a Galapagos t-shirt, and 16 CDs with all of our pictures transferred to them. He passed the pictures around and we all were impressed once again with the vast variety we had seen of birds, iguanas, tortoises, mammals, and sea life.

But now it was time to announce who won the treasure hunt. After all the pictures circulated, he pulled out three of them and taped them to the window.

"Okay, mis amigos y amigas, the captain and I need to know who shot each of these three pictures." The first was a nest of eggs with two blue-footed boobies standing nearby, cautiously watching the photographer. The second was a picture of two enormous lounging sea lions with a baby sea lion between them. And the last was a faraway picture of an albatross falling off its cliff and taking flight, and you could see that just below it on the cliff was a bird's nest.

We all looked at each other silently for a moment and then a small voice from the back of the room answered, "I did. Did I do something wrong?"

"No, Timmy, you did something remarkable," Juan congratulated him. "You captured the essence and the special treasure of the Galapagos Islands in all three pictures. Those of us who live and work here are taking care of these islands so that all of these animals have a future. And every time these animals have babies, that is a treasure beyond any value for them and for us. Timmy, you found and recorded those treasures with these nesting pictures, so you win the treasure hunt and this special Galapagos t-shirt. We all hope you'll come back again one day when you have children of your own and share with them the treasures you discovered here."

So, as it turned out, all of the adults on this tour learned something important from this child. We were introduced to the history, geology, and biology of the Galapagos Islands and discovered and explored a remarkable diversity of living animals and protected land and oceans. We also realized we had learned an important lesson about what is important in this place as well as elsewhere on our planet: the preservation of our animal and plant neighbors is as important as the preservation of our own human species.

Author's epilogue: Lonesome George, the last Pinta Island tortoise, died without a mate or offspring on June 24, 2012, four years after my trip, and now his species is considered extinct. Timmy went on to UCLA with a full scholarship and now is an environmental biologist with a national nonprofit environmental organization.

Ronald Javor lives in Sacramento and spent his legal career assisting people with low incomes, disabilities, and homelessness to access safe and affordable housing. Since "retirement", Ron volunteers his time continuing the same work as well as advocating for environmental justice. He also continues his writing, interspersed with travel and camping.

Ron has written seven children's books on young people confronting and overcoming these barriers. Each book addresses negative stereotypes and shows that all children, despite their handicaps, have the same goals and desires. His recently published Young Adult book, *Our Forever Home*, features Loneome George, the extinct Galapagos tortoise, and Dodo, an extinct bird, exploring the past and present worlds of extinct animals now living in Our Forever Home, the effects of climate change, and what can be done about climate change to save today's animals, including humans. More information is available on his books at ronaldjavorbooks.com

BACKYARD PARADISE

DAVE TODD

"Nature bats last." Richard Feynman, the famous physicist, said that. He was right.

I've always considered Yosemite National Park to be my backyard. I live in Sacramento now, but I spend every chance I get in Yosemite. I've cross-country skied across the Sierra Nevada through Yosemite sixteen times, most recently in 2019. I've witnessed the recession of the glaciers due to climate change in real time.

My first trans-Sierra trip was in 1996. I had been cross-country skiing for eighteen years at that point. I had skied to Ostrander Lake (twenty miles round trip) and Glacier Point (twenty-one miles round trip) in Yosemite National Park several times. As a member of the Nordic Ski Patrol, I would ski out Glacier Point Road just about every other weekend. I would spend the night between Washburn Point and Glacier Point. In the morning, I would look out the bedroom window and watch the sun rise behind Half Dome. Those trips where demanding, but only a prelude to what I encountered on the trans-Sierra trips (forty-two miles).

The Yosemite Winter Cross Country Ski Club sponsors trips to Ostrander Lake, Glacier Point, Tuolumne Meadows, and across the Sierra. The trans-Sierra trips begin with a flight over the Sierra to the Mono Lake International Airport. Actually, it's just an asphalt strip. Once we unload our ski gear and back packs from the plane, we catch a ride to the gate on Tioga Pass Road several miles west of Lee Vining. The gate is locked all winter long. Sometimes the road closes as early as October and doesn't reopen until May or even June. It can also close due to snow any month of the year.

179

Because the gate is locked, we usually hike up the road five or more miles to wherever the snowline is. Then we gear up with our skis and backpacks and start skiing up Tioga Road (Hwy 120) several miles west of Lee Vining and Hwy 395. It's about eight miles from the locked gate to the east entrance of Yosemite National Park. There are certain parts of the road that are especially avalanche prone. We spread out about twenty-five feet apart in those locations. Often, we encounter large boulders and rocks that have fallen off the mountain and onto the road. Once, three French skiers were swept off the road by a small avalanche. Fortunately, they were not injured. They were able to climb back up to the road.

Tioga Pass is at the 9,943-foot elevation. From that point it's mostly level skiing to the east entrance of Yosemite National Park. We spend our first night there.

The second day is a long one. We ski gradually uphill for eight miles past brooding and majestic snow-covered peaks. Eventually we descend into Tuolumne Meadows. We have stayed in various locations there including Parson's Memorial Lodge, the McCauley Cabin, the gas station operated by the park concessionaire, fitted out with bunkbeds in the wintertime, and more recently at the visitor's center which becomes the cross-country ski hut in the winter, open first-come-first-served to the public.

After an overnight stay, we sometimes ski to the top of Lembert Dome, which is a granite rock formation at the 9,455-foot elevation that soars 800 feet above the meadows and the Tuolumne River. All of Tuolumne Meadows and the surrounding peaks and domes are visible from that point. On my most recent trip there, I saw a very rare Pacific Fisher (a small mammal from the weasel family) run across the road by the bridge over the Tuolumne River. It's fairly unusual for us to see wildlife on the north side of the valley in the wintertime. The coyotes used to greet me when I would return from patrolling Glacier Point Road, but I've never seen one on the trans-Sierra trip. To get water we either melt snow, or drop a bucket on a rope into the river. Sometimes, we have to chop through the ice to get water from the river.

We usually spend two nights in Tuolumne Meadows. That allows time for side trips to Glenn Aulin, Florence Lake, Budd Lake, and Pot Hole Dome. On one trip, I discovered that both of my ski boots had split at the toe. Another member's skis had delaminated and were split horizontally down the middle. Our trip leader saved the day. He had brought *Barge Cement* and duct tape. He poured *Barge Cement* into the split toes and bound them up with duct tape. He applied the same remedy to the delaminated skis and held them together with vise grips. Both the boots and the skis were ready to use in the morning. The repairs lasted for the rest of the trip.

We cache our food in bear lockers outside the cabins where we stay in the fall. We eat well on these trips. There is a different menu for each meal and each day of the trip. I've made lemon meringue pies and other specialty items on the trips.

The approximately twelve miles from Tuolumne Meadows to Snow Flat on the next-to-last day is the longest section that we ski. Usually, we ski across Tenaya Lake if it is frozen solid. It's a mile long and surrounded by granite peaks and domes. We spread out twenty-five feet apart as a precaution. I've skied across the lake during a winter storm under white-out conditions. On other trips, I've skied under bright sunshine that was almost hot. It's all uphill from Tenaya Lake past the May Lake turnoff to Snow Flat where we stay for the night.

Snow Flat is a magical place to stay. Mount Hoffman is not far from the cabin and sometimes skiers who are not exhausted from the trip ski up the mountain. In 1997, I answered a call of nature in the middle of the night. As I returned from the outhouse approximately twenty feet from my sleeping bag, I looked up. There, framed between two mountains, I saw the Hale-Bopp comet. It was a magical, once in a life time experience, and there was no one to share it with. Since cell phones with cameras hadn't been perfected and my Canon SLR was in my backpack, I am left only with the memory of the sight.

The last day of the trip is all cross country – a ten-mile descent to Mirror Lake in the valley and the backpacker parking lot. We ski down the hill, cross Tioga Pass Road and past an abandoned rock quarry. Then it's out to what we have christened Serendipity Point from which we have a cinematic view of Cloud's Rest and Half Dome. Usually, we have lunch there at one of the finest outdoor dining areas in the country. After lunch we ski downhill until we reach the forest below.

I contributed the following story to "Inspiring Generations" published by the Yosemite Conservancy. On one trip I noticed that one of our skiers wasn't with the group. My friend Phil and I turned around and skied back for thirty minutes. We found her hanging upside down in a tree well by her ski tips. Then I was faced with a moral dilemma. Take a picture, or rescue her. We rescued her...but I still wish I had the picture.

A mile beyond Serendipity Point, we follow the trail which wends past the Snow Creek Ski Hut, which was built in the 1920s. At that time the concessionaire planned to build a series of ski huts based on the European model. Other than the Snow Creek Ski Hut and the ski hut at Ostrander Lake, the plan was never completed due to World War II. The first time I saw the hut, the original furnishings and vintage ski posters were still inside. Later the park service removed those items for preservation. Now the hut is open by reservation to skiers and snowshoers in the winter.

The final leg of the trip begins not far from the Snow Creek Hut with a ski run down Herringbone Hill to the snowline. The hike down the Snow Creek Trail eventually ends behind Mirror Lake on the valley floor. You can imagine the hike down as the hand of nature gradually revealing the infinite beauty of our planet. A mass of green on the valley floor slowly reveals individual trees. The types of trees change from pines to oaks as we descend. Depending on the weather and the snow year, we pass many streams fed by snow melt that cross the trail. All varieties of wild flowers and mushrooms are there in abundance. After we finally reach the valley floor, it's another two-mile hike to the stables where our cars are normally parked.

One year the trail to Mirror Lake had disappeared. An avalanche of huge trees and boulders that had fallen the previous September blocked the path. It was possible to wend our way between them, but we were only able to accomplish it with the aid of another friend who had already made the passage and called out instructions to us.

We part company at the parking lot. Then the long drive to our separate homes around the state begins. One year I couldn't remember the correct trail to the parking lot. I stopped various tourists to ask them for help. None knew where the stables were. The battery in my headlamp was growing dim. I was about to give up and set up my tent to spend the night on the valley floor when my battery went dead. Just then a young couple walked up the path from the opposite direction. I went to them and said, "Can you help me? I'm lost." They smiled and said, "You're one block from the Ahwahnee Hotel." Sometimes men do ask for directions.

During one summer work party we volunteered to scrape the paint off one of the high-country cabins and repaint it. We also cleaned and sanitized the interior. At another work party we cut and split eighteen cords of firewood for Parson's Memorial Lodge, and picked up litter on the trails in Tuolumne Meadows. Due to the pandemic and the closure of the high-country cabins by the National Park Service, there have been no ski trips by the ski club in Yosemite since March, 2020. I will be ready to ski again, through my backyard paradise, when they have re-opened.

Dave Todd served at Fort MacArthur, California and Flak Kaserne, Augsburg Germany in the US Army, and now lives in Sacramento, California working in water use efficiency for the State of California.

A birth defect in his right hip kept Dave out of sports until he was ten, but now he surfs, has skied across the Sierra sixteen times and to Ostrander Lake and Glacier Point in Yosemite. He hikes the Sierra almost every other weekend, and last year hiked the Haute Route (high road), eighty miles through the Alps from Mont Blanc to the Matterhorn.

Dave has produced *The Nitty Gritty (Down N' Dirty) Landscape and Garden Club* for public television, and the *Project Water Works* for the American Water Works Association. He also wrote *Sibling Rivalry,* and contributed two stories to *Inspiring Generations* published by the Yosemite Conservancy.

website: https://www.wordwrangler.me.
email: davetodd@mac.com.

Glacier Point, Yosemite National Park

THE BERMUDA TRIANGLE— DESTINATION NASSAU

BARBARA KLIDE

A LOOK BACK TO 1965
The Triangle

The Bermuda Triangle has a legendary history with thousands of ships having sunk to the bottom of the North Atlantic Ocean. Some ships were eventually found, their crew missing. Aircraft simply disappeared, including a group of five US Navy bombers on a training mission in 1945.

A physical anomaly, the Bermuda Triangle is one of only two places on Earth where a compass points to true north rather than magnetic north. It is a scalene triangle with slightly uneven sides located between Bermuda, Miami, and San Juan, and includes some of the world's most travelled shipping lanes for private and commercial vessels and planes heading for global ports including in the Americas.

Also known as the Devil's Triangle, a cult of extraterrestrial and paranormal claims grew from those incidents, but the following two stories have neither to blame. One is a story of weather, screw-ups, and sheer luck or the near-miss versus accident phenomena; the other, a story of screw-ups, lax international law, Murphy's Law, or perhaps it was the triangle.

"The Fun Ship"

In the 1960s, the number one port of call was Nassau. It is the capital of the Bahamas, a member of the British Commonwealth and located 180 miles southeast of Miami within the left corner of the Bermuda Triangle.

The first story finds a ship limping into Nassau's Prince George Wharf Port several days late of its scheduled arrival–its travelers depleted and desperate to reach land. Their "pleasure" cruise began at the New York Passenger Ship Terminal on the Hudson River on a day in August 1965. Among the passengers was a small family consisting of two parents, a boy who had just turned 16, and a girl (this author) who would be turning 15 not long after.

The second story, barely three months later, was when a ship left the Port of Miami on a Friday, likewise a pleasure cruise destined for Nassau. But, in the early hours of the next day, November 13, its journey ended in one of the worst shipwrecks recorded in the Americas. The *SS Yarmouth Castle* caught fire and sank in over 10,000 feet in the Bermuda Triangle. Both ships were one and the same.

∞

It should be noted that according to sailors, one of the most superstitious groups that may have ever existed, two cardinal rules must be followed: you never sail on a Friday and never, ever change the ship's name. Those two rules were broken. There are other such rules, but I specifically ruled out never to board a ship if you just saw a redhead.

∞

Back in NYC, our parents were beguiled by a colorful oceangoing vacation brochure boasting "The Fun Ship" with a newly built on-deck pool, 100% air conditioning throughout, glassed-in promenade deck, teakwood cabins, a luxurious dining room, and a gambling casino with flourishes of flocked wallpaper—a nod to an older era.

We'd be about two days en route—the steamship travelled only 21 miles per hour. We'd then spend three glorious days in Nassau, and finally return after another two days at sea.

A day after departure, our ship, the *SS Yarmouth Castle*, was caught in a cyclone, which was recorded as a tropical depression, an "unnamed TD". Had the maximum sustained windspeed exceeded 39 miles per hours, the United Nation's World Meteorological Organization would have upgraded the storm according to its wind scale, and bestowed it a proper name like Katrina, Andrew, Sandy, or Betsy.

As the no-name TD crept up on us, my brother Robert and I were swimming with abandon in the new pool and quickly found out why heavy maritime ropes had been fastened along its walls. As the powerful swells began bouncing the ship around, we grabbed onto the ropes while the pool water swept away from the cabin side splashing barrels of water out to the ocean. We were having the time of our lives laughing and dangling over the empty side until Mom appeared issuing a blood-curdling command with perfect enunciation befitting an army drill sergeant, "GET OUT OF THE POOL NOW." We obeyed.

Back in our cabin, our parents were speaking in hushed voices. We managed to clean up and dress for dinner not knowing that we would be having the last supper of the trip. In the dining room we watched passengers flee their tables, trying to make it to the bathroom as the onslaught of waves lashed the ship. We fled as well.

Looking out the tiny cabin porthole window, we saw the towering waves washing across the deck. In between the crashing waves there was silence. The ship's engine had ceased.

With a brief reprieve from infirmity, Robert and I slipped through the door and wandered the ship for another stupid, fearless teen adventure, pulling ourselves along the wall railings. In their condition, our parents didn't even try to stop us. Dad wore a towel over his head.

We reached the now-empty dining room where the chairs and uncleared tables of half-eaten food were freakishly sliding around amidst a taint in the air. We were enveloped in a spine-chilling Twilight Zone moment sending us scrambling back to our parents to find them gripping their bedsheets. There were no cabin straps to help keep us securely in place.

Periodically a crew member would knock on our cabin door with news...we were miles off course, the engine was being repaired, an SOS was sent to the U.S. Coast Guard—they were unable to help. More knocks and we were told that the TD had come through the Bermuda Triangle and up to where we were languishing due east of South Carolina and due west of Bermuda. The last knocks delivered word that the doctor was missing, and oh, yes, there was a knifing on board. We never heard if the victim lived or died. We knew the crew was comprised of international staff and apparently a couple of them had a tiff. And after first boarding, we never again saw our young, handsome, Greek captain.

The incessant, monster waves tortured us for over two days. We struggled to get from our beds to the bathroom and back again, praying for sleep.

We woke up on the third day to the sound of gentle, rolling waves lapping against the ship, the kind that would rock a baby to sleep. More importantly we heard the unmistakable sound of the ship's engine. The skies were still gray, but the worst was over. It was not the fun ship of which the brochure boasted.

Destination Nassau

We arrived to a brilliant, sunny island paradise, Nassau, just when we were scheduled to make the return trip, but the majestic, aging *SS Yarmouth Castle* was still being patched up. No matter, we were never to board her again.

My brother and I did not trouble ourselves with the minutia of cruise refunds, discussions about the engine conking out, or the scoop on the knifing. We left that wrangling up to our parents.

What trickled down to us was that either the cruise line's modus operandi was one of low risk aversion, defying Murphy's Law, or that no one has power over the ocean.

Getting back home was another concern to which Robert and I paid no mind. We only had eyes for the motorbikes which were rented to anyone who could turn the key and reach the pedals, much to the dismay of Mom who cried, arguing with Dad about this half-baked idea. Dad respectfully listened to his beloved whose wailings tugged deeply at our hearts, but we wanted what we wanted, arguing with teen passion how competent we were.

Dad delivered the final say allowing us to "go play". I treasure the memory of both Mom's emotional torrent for the safety of us kids and Dad's willingness to expose us to new experiences. Dad was the one who taught us how to ride a bike and was confident we'd be okay. Mom still saw us as her babies.

I trusted my older brother to lead the way and we eventually arrived back in one piece to our new digs, the Princess Hotel, after a day of intrepid teen spirit. Our frontal lobes were not completely wired yet to grasp the full concept of fear to the extent that Mom displayed.

As a footnote, the Princess Hotel later suffered a fire and spate of hurricanes. It was left to rot on acres of land with nothing salvageable and can be seen on Google satellite with walls collapsed. Once a destination, today it remains a looted archeological-like site.

Detour to 60's Miami

We wound up enjoying an extended stay in palm tree-filled Nassau before Dad arranged to fly us to Miami. There, we got checked into an overbooked *Fontainebleau Hotel* after Dad pulled strings with a gracious man who had been patronizing his Manhattan jewelry store which Dad owned a total of 35 years.

*   *   *

The store was on East 59th Street between Park and Madison Avenues on the ground level in what was then called the Delmonico Hotel and now Trump Park Avenue with a history of milestones including Bob Dylan meeting the Beatles a year earlier and sharing a joint.

Dad met scores of movie stars like Barbra Streisand,

politicians, the Archbishop of New York, the local police, and even Khrushchev when his people learned that our grandfather worked at the store and spoke Russian. That's where he also befriended Lester, the Fontainebleau Hotel's concierge.

Where once pedestrians saw sparkling, spotlighted, and breathtakingly beautiful jewelry resting on velvet pads through plate glass windows, today one could only see people on exercise bikes in a gym that took over and expanded Dad's space.

∞

First-class and swanky, the *Fontainebleau* was part of a bygone era and Frank Sinatra's favorite hotel. Movies were filmed there, including Sinatra's own and a James Bond classic, *Goldfinger*, released in 1964. And in yet another Bond movie, *Dr. No,* our "Fun ship" can be seen in the background with its former name, Evangeline, painted on its bow. It was renamed the *SS Yarmouth Castle* just a year earlier when it changed hands.

Sinatra was performing nightly to a sold-out house at the *Fontainebleau's* La Ronde Supper Club the week we arrived, and Lester couldn't swing tickets for us. Other shows were available, and to keep the kids occupied, the hotel had a downstairs discotheque where the juke box was free.

I put on my British "mod" mini dress; my hair done up in the original teased beehive perfectly resurrected decades later by Amy Winehouse. Robert was in his shiny long-sleeved shirt, the costume of all his bandmates in a rock and roll group originally called the "4 Notes" and later the groovy, "The Electrons." We danced away the night with other kids, until our parents came to collect us.

Mom, an American beauty, wore a sleeveless sequined-cropped top and satin ankle length skirt with a slit to her knee. Dad looked sharp in his pressed white shirt and a deep navy-blue sport coat, clip-on silk bowtie (worn daily in his shop) and light taupe slacks, handsome in spite of a broken nose that he never got fixed from a "practice" boxing bout with Kid Chocolate in Cuba before the real fight took place. Kid Chocolate swept the ring with Dad when the original practice boxer had come down with food poisoning. Dad, a one-time local Golden Gloves winner, was the ill-fated substituted recruit, but that's a 1930s story for another time.

When not at the hotel's beach or the pool, we spent our days visiting the sights and sounds of Miami, including the *Art Deco Historic District*, the *Vizcaya Museum and Gardens*, and the alligator-infested waters for an airboat ride in the *Everglades National Park*.

The Triangle comes Full Circle

Our family, returned to NY by air, went about its business –Dad working in the city, Robert and I returning to school, and Mom, once a CBS administrative assistant, then tending our small apartment in Jackson Heights, Queens.

One Saturday morning, the radio blasted news that the *SS Yarmouth Castle* had sunk in the Bermuda Triangle. Sitting in front of our new color TV we watched the story unfold. As teens, we were old enough to recognize the significance—that it could have been us. Maybe our first fear of doom at sea combined with an eerie "close call" kicked our frontal lobes into full maturity, sending the second real chill of our lives down our spines.

SS Yarmouth Castle: Tragedy, backstory and legacy

Eighty-seven souls on board the *SS Yarmouth Castle* died when the ship caught fire on its way to Nassau. She burned on a clear night and just after 6:00 a.m. capsized and sank, taking the passengers to the bottom of the Atlantic with her. Fortunately, some 459 people were rescued by a cruiser, *Bahama Star,* and a Finnish freighter, *Finnpulp*. Both ships turned back from their own journeys to different Bahama ports across the Triangle when the stricken ship went missing on their radar. They were heroes.

Built in Philadelphia in 1927, the ship was christened *Evangeline* and along with a sister ship named *Yarmouth*, the two ships had storied adventures if not muddled histories carrying cargo in their early years, troops during World War II, and taking on various jobs overseas before being consigned to cruising duties. The sisters changed hands several times and confusingly changed names each using "*Yarmouth*" at one time or another; the name associated with townships in both Nova Scotia and Massachusetts.

The *SS Yarmouth Castle* – our "Fun Ship" -- has been written about in dozens of articles and in 2015, on the 50th anniversary of the sinking, more articles published resurrecting the story and the account of the disgraced captain. As such, I recount only key information.

∞

Located above the boiler room, stateroom 610 was too hot for passengers so it was used to store mattresses which were stacked close to the ceiling light. Why the fire erupted that night, on this trip is unknown; arson was suspected, but could not be proven.

The blaze rapidly spread through the ship. The *SS Yarmouth Castle*, registered at that time under the Panamanian flag, was not under the jurisdiction of the U.S. Coast Guard (USCG) with more stringent conventions than international law. The USCG subsequently undertook an investigation and determined that the ship had multiple missteps including negligence exacerbated by the captain himself, the same man who captained our cruise.

In a 27-page report the USCG found that there were no sprinklers in the stateroom, there were excessive layers of never-stripped wall paint, painted ropes so hard they kept some lifeboats from launching, porthole clamps painted over, locking the windows shut, no fire doors were closed, life jackets were missing, inflatable life rafts were not on board, and evacuation procedures were never presented to the passengers.

The captain and other of the crew were charged with violation of duty. They had left the ship before trying to rescue their passengers, arguing that they were just seeking help. There were, however, accounts of crew valor where some took off their own life vests and gave them to people in their charge.

As a result of the tragedy, the Safety of Life at Sea law (SOLAS), was heavily revamped adding maritime fire drills and mandating the use of non-combustible material like steel in ship construction.

Public relations surrounding the disaster precluded the surviving sister ship from operating successfully. She struggled for about a decade under several more owners and names until she was finally scrapped in Greece in 1977.

Redeeming value

Separate from our harrowing weather assault, when the SS Yarmouth's safety deficiencies emerged, we realized that we were unknowingly cruising with the same ones and experienced a near-miss versus the accident of the later cruise. However, if a fire had broken out during the cyclone we surely would have perished—there could be no rescue ships to save us. No telling why we were lucky, but when answers eluded us, we were left grateful to have been north of the Bermuda Triangle rather than caught up within its devilry.

Near miss versus accident is the consequence of Murphy's Law which has its roots in science and mathematics—it's often tossed about as a humorous expression, but it is a reasoned observation and scientific law that arose from the military community. It involves considering all the possibilities, testing and countering them, or pay the consequences. Murphy's Law famously stated means, "Everything that can possibly go wrong will go wrong." It is just a matter of time. Perhaps this reminder to us is the redeeming value of these two incidents.

The Panamanian company had low risk aversion. The safety of their passengers was not their top priority. They took a chance with the *SS Yarmouth Castle* and eventually lax thoughtlessness led to tragedy...or the combined circumstances were set in motion by the anomaly of the Bermuda Triangle.

*   *   *

Two years after the disaster, Gordon Lightfoot a well-known folk singer of the day composed the Ballad of the Yarmouth Castle. In these lyrics there is a consequence of neglect, all too awful, but one not to ignore:
"...But the sands run out within her heart
A tiny spark glows red
It smolders through the evening...
...She burned all through the night
Then slipped 'neath the waves
In the mornin'".

In Memory of...

...the passengers who perished on November 13, 1965 – GPS Latitude: 25° 55' 0.12" N, Longitude: -78° 5' 60" W, and my mom and dad who now rest in peace (2004 and 2010 respectively) in North Lauderdale five miles from the *Yarmouth Castle Memorial* in Pompano Beach, Florida.

And Dedicated to...
Robert, a great brother who contributed two recollections of his own; the last supper and Dad's towel.

Barbara Klide was born in New York City and graduated with an MBA from Golden Gate University, San Francisco, and a Certificate in Graphic Design from the University of California, Davis. She retired in 2022 after 28 years as the Director of Marketing for Quest Technology Management, California.

It was at this firm where she was presented the opportunity for discovery of the mated pair of elegant, sensitive and smart Canada Geese and their goslings who nested several years in a row in the corporate courtyard. Her skills in observation and compassion, coupled with writing and photography allowed her to bring this amazing story to others who also find interest and excitement about wildlife in our midst. The first two years of the story are captured in *Secret Lives of Wild Canada Geese* published in 2022.

Her early writings about this remarkable pair and their offspring drew much interest from several including Dr. Lorin Lindner, PhD, *Wolves and Warriors*, (Animal Planet) and Bill Bianco, President, Audubon Society, Sacramento. Barbara donates book profits to various wildlife rescue groups.

Barbara is also a contributing author to several anthologies published by the Northern California Publishers and Authors Association (NCPA) including *Destination: The World Volumes One and Two, All Holidays 2020 and 2021, and More Birds of a Feather*.

For more information and photos, visit BarbaraKlide.com or BijouPublishing.com

THE SACRAMENTO: RIVER OF GOLD

CHERYL ANNE STAPP

At 447 miles in length, the Sacramento River is the longest river that flows through California, with a watershed that encompasses more than 27,000 square miles. Some say it is the mightiest and most important river in the state. Yet—in human eyes at least— its origins are humble: a steady trickle that ripples over small rocks near majestic Mount Shasta, within today's Mount Shasta City Park.

Originally glacier melt from a long-ago epoch, the headwaters spring from Big Springs Aquifer, an underground body of porous rock, after more than fifty years of filtration through volcanic rock, before exiting through the side of Big Springs Hill. From an initial north-east course, the river turns south, through glades of ferns, wild azaleas and mountain meadows. It flows in and out of Lake Shasta and through forests of fir, pine, spruce and cedar. Below Red Bluff the river enters the Sacramento Valley, coursing through low hills and flat grasslands. Along the way hundreds of springs and creeks spill into the river, and the Sacramento further swells in volume as each of its principal tributaries, the Pit, the McCloud, the Feather and the American, converge with its flow.

Meandering through the expansive, inland California Delta and estuary, it meets the San Joaquin River, ripples through Suisun and San Pablo bays, the Carquinez Strait and San Francisco Bay, and flows on through the Golden Gate to join the Pacific Ocean. The indigenous Native Americans lived and traded along this river for thousands of years. The first outsiders to actually explore, and realize the river's breadth and power, were Spanish explorer Gabriel Moraga and his crew in 1808. Moraga named it *Rios de los*

Sacramentos, "River of the Blessed Sacrament."

During the California Gold Rush, the Sacramento River was a busy highway trafficked by steamships and smaller watercraft, transporting prospectors to the upland mines and freighting their gold back to San Francisco banks. Then it was called "the river of gold," navigable from San Francisco to Marysville, although during floods, steamships might chance going as far upriver as Red Bluff.

The river-highway was dangerous then. Haste was an imperative to eager gold-rushers, who wanted to get to the gold fields in a hurry. The wonder of boiler-stoked steamboat speed, as opposed to slower-moving sailing vessels, became the dominant mode of river travel. But the mechanisms of steam-fueled watercraft held inherent risks—and for some less than responsible ship captains, the opportunity for an amusing one-upmanship contest.

Such a contest developed when the steamship *Pearl*'s captain bet cigars with his crew that he could outrun the *Enterprise* coming alongside them as both vessels were returning downstream from Marysville on January 27, 1855. The flaming explosion of the *Pearl*'s over-wrought boiler could be heard thirteen blocks distant from the mouth of the American River at Sacramento City, where the disaster occurred.

Boatmen trolled the water for days, finally recovering seventy bodies that were laid out in a public building in hopes of being recognized. Few were claimed, although the remains of the Pearl's captain and members of his crew were identified. Meanwhile, the town held a public funeral on January 29 for the upwards of forty victims already recovered. Three thousand people, including seven hundred Chinese mourning their eighteen dead, attended the solemn ceremony.

The river itself suffered the consequences of the Gold Rush. Eventually, debris from hydraulic mining operations raised the river's bed so high that by the late nineteenth century, large ships could go no farther upstream than the city of Sacramento.

Although native bird populations on the river have

declined since the nineteenth century, today the river supports 135 species of native birds including egrets, great blue herons, and bald eagles. Nearly sixty species of fish—among them bass, trout, salmon and steelhead—live in the Sacramento River, offering seasonal year-round fishing opportunities for anglers. Campers, fishermen and day-trippers may also spot otters, beavers, gray fox, bobcat, a variety of reptiles and amphibians, and western pond turtles.

Occasionally, marine animals wander into the Sacramento River looking for food or refuge, and get lost. Sea lions, for example, have been seen and rescued from places far inland.

Whales, of course, are another matter. Two "lost whale" dramas have played out fairly recently, completely enthralling the general public. In 1985 a lone humpback whale, affectionately dubbed "Humphrey" by the media, traveled 69 miles up the Sacramento River. In 2007 two humpback whales, thought to be a mother and her calf, swam even farther upstream, to the vicinity of the deep-water ship channel at West Sacramento. All three creatures were eventually coaxed back to the Pacific Ocean, safe and sound, through the efforts of the Marine Mammal Center and the United States Coast Guard.

As rivers go, the Sacramento is considered young, perhaps only three million years old. Does the once-celebrated "river of gold" have any gold of its own? The Sacramento flows well west of California's rich gold regions; but, after all, it *is* fed by the Feather River and the American River, both gold-bearing streams. Be that as it may—given its distance from regional gold sources, plus the Sacramento's swift-moving current—if present, the mineral would be as finely textured as sand and widely diffused, not worth the cost and effort to prospect. So far, from the nineteenth century great Gold Rush era to the present, no one has tried.

 Cheryl Anne Stapp writes nonfiction California history. A native Sacramentan, she graduated from California State University, Northridge; during her last five years in Los Angeles, she was a contributing editor to *Working World*, a regional magazine. Returning home in 2000, Cheryl lives with her husband in Sacramento—in bygone days, an important Gold Rush town. Her titles have won awards from the Next Generation Indie Awards and the Independent Press Awards. Website "California's Olden Golden Days" at http://www.CherylAnneStapp.com/

She is the author of *Wild Wicked Woman – The Life of a Gold Rush Courtesan*; *Rise, Ruin & Restoration – A History of Sutter's Fort*; *Before the Gold Rush - The Sinclairs of Rancho del Paso 1840-1849*; *Disaster & Triumph: Sacramento Women, Gold Rush Through the Civil War*; *Sacramento Chronicles - A Golden Past*, and *The Stagecoach in Northern California: Rough Rides, Gold Camps, and Daring Drivers*.

CRACK IN THE EARTH

ELLEN OSBORN

Several years back my husband and I bought our first Jeep and wanted to give it a good trial. We were eager to get it muddy and see what it could do. A magazine article I had read labeled Highway 50 through the state of Nevada as the "Loneliest Highway in the United States." That sounded good for the Jeep's first adventure. We loaded it up with luggage, and armed with a list of roadside attractions, started out, leaving the comforts of our Los Altos home.

We stopped at an almost deserted ghost town for lunch, then visited the crumbling ruins of an adobe Pony Express remount station. While we were there, a sudden summer downpour gave the Jeep a baptism in mud. After stopping for every historical marker, we saw - no, we didn't pass up a single one! - we ended up for the night in the town of Ely, Nevada, near the Utah border. The next day we took a ride on a newly restored steam train and visited a copper mine. From there we headed back to California, stopping to hunt for garnets on a desert hillside. Apparently, that took a skill we didn't have, not to mention the right tools, so we didn't find any.

We were down to the last roadside (or in this case, off road) attraction on our list: *The Crack in the Earth.* According to the magazine article the crack was caused by one of five major earthquakes that occurred in that part of Nevada between July and December of 1954, causing much property damage and some injuries. As Bay Area residents, we had experienced a few earthquakes, so we were always interested in earthquake activity.

We figured we could just squeeze that in before stopping for the night. We found the correct turn-off and began the drive to the *Crack in the Earth*. The pavement ended about two car lengths from the highway. No matter – we had a Jeep! Bouncing along on a faintly discernable track in the dirt, we continued on, confident of finding the last and most remote item on our itinerary. The sun was dipping low in the west, a time to be heading out of the desert, not in. Lights had come on in some farmhouses far off to our left in the valley below. This was pretty empty country.

We were both craning our necks, looking for some sign that we were nearing the *Crack in the Earth*. Suddenly, off to our right we spotted a lone kitchen chair, the kind popular in the 1940s, made of steel tubing with a cracked and faded red vinyl seat and back. Propped on the seat was a hand-lettered sign reading *"Crack in the Earth"* with an arrow pointing into the weeds on our right. There was no evidence of anyone ever driving there, but off we went, heading toward the setting sun. Shortly thereafter we spotted a single, rusty Buick hubcap nestled in the tumbleweeds and sagebrush. Considering it was taking my husband's full attention to keep the Jeep upright while steering around and over rocks, I was filled with admiration for the Buick driver's skill and daring.

A little farther on we were confronted by an abrupt low ridge blocking forward progress. Still intent on finding the promised *Crack in the Earth*, with full faith in the advice of the vinyl kitchen chair, my husband put the Jeep in its lowest gear and attacked the nearly perpendicular wall of dirt. With the engine roaring, the wheels spouting dust, up we went. I was terrified. I expected the Jeep to turn over with us trapped inside right there in the middle of nowhere. Nobody knew where we were. We could die a slow and painful death pinned under the wreckage of our new Jeep! The Jeep quickly slipped out of gear and we slid backwards. Undaunted, my husband worked the gears and tried again. He was really in his element, enjoying the challenge. I hid in the only place I could – the pages of a novel I had been reading. I really preferred not to know what was happening. More engine roar, more dust clouding our vision, and again we slid backwards. It's good to know when you're licked, and we clearly were.

My husband carefully backed up the now scratched and dirty Jeep, turned around and we headed back to Highway 50, hoping to make it out before full dark. The comforts of dinner at a roadhouse and a night in a motel bed sounded pretty good by then. Neither one of us spoke, but we were both thinking maybe the sign on the vinyl kitchen chair was somebody's idea of a joke. Then I happened to look back in the rearview mirror. Through a coating of fine desert dust, I looked at the ridge that had defeated us. Then in the long shadows of dusk I saw it – we had been in the *Crack in the Earth*! The ridge was one side of it. The passing decades had softened the edges and covered it with scrub brush, but it was still there, a memorial to the terrifying events that caused the surface of the earth to rupture and reshape the landscape.

Ever since that trip, when a roadside attraction fails to live up to its promise, we call it another *Crack in the Earth*. It was worth the trip because we still laugh about it. In later years as devoted Jeepers, we often found ourselves alone in the middle of nowhere, listening to the howl of coyotes, and blazing our own way through the wilds. I never again lost faith in our Jeep or my husband's judgement.

Primarily a writer of nonfiction history, Ellen is the author of the recently released history of El Dorado County, *A Lovely And Comfortable Heritage Lost.* She has also written more than 20 historical articles for such periodicals as *Sierra Heritage, Around Here* and the *Overland Journal.* She has contributions in NCPA's five previous anthologies, *Our Dance With Words, Birds of a Feather Vols. I and II,* and *Destination The World Vols. I and II.* A member of the Placerville Shakespeare Club, she helped research and write the well-received original presentation "El Dorado's True Gold Notable Women's Stories" in 2013.

Ellen is a member of the El Dorado Writer's Guild and Northern California Publishers and Authors. She can be reached at slyparkbooks@gmail.com

A fourth generation Californian, Ellen graduated from San Francisco State. After spending her work life in the Bay Area, she and her husband are now retired and live in Pollock Pines, CA.

ALTITUDE ADJUSTMENT

BARBARA YOUNG

I can still remember the way I felt when I summited Fitzpatrick Peak. My friend Holt had invited me to his home state of Colorado. I was excited about the adventure because we would hike on the Continental Divide, to an altitude higher than I had ever hiked. The peak was his favorite *13er*, one over 13,000 feet in elevation.

At the time I lived on St. John, an island in the Caribbean. Because I travelled from sea level, we needed to allow time for me to acclimatize to the altitude before venturing up onto the Divide. We stayed the first night at just over 4500 feet in Grand Junction.

Our second night was at 9222 feet in Pitkin, a scant settlement of hunting cabins. We had a cozy night of sleep by the fireplace aglow, under the watchful eyes of elk and deer mounted on the walls—all trophies of his family's sport.

The following morning, we packed our backpacks with our own clothing, sleeping bag and foam pad. The items-in-common, such as tent, stove, fuel, food and water, were divvied up. There was no need for any hair care products. My mid-back length hair would stay in a braid for the next several days. No need for make-up either, but lotion and lip moisturizer were important skin protection from the dry and cold. A pocket camera, small notebook and star chart were my personal items. No phone, no GPS—just a map, compass, binoculars and whistle because that's how it was done in the early 1990s.

Later, a short drive from the village, we started our hike through the dense forest of quaking golden aspens, on an overgrown roadside trail. Our goal that afternoon was simply to gain altitude. We set our camp amidst a small patch of fir trees on the western side of the Divide at about 9600 feet.

When I awoke the next morning, I instinctually paused my breathing so I could listen deeper into the serenity. The thin material of the tent was subtly illuminated by dawn. Shadowed by the mountain, we had slept later than planned.

Holt awoke growling like a bear as he stretched. "D'you hear that?"

No, but I hadn't given any thought to bears. What could he be referring to?

Then, a faint, *shhh-pft.*

He bounced his left index finger into the tent material overhead.

Again, louder. *SHHH-PHHHFFFT.*

"That's snow sliding off the tent," he said with a brightness in his voice, as if he magically made it snow overnight.

My curiosity to see the new fallen snow motivated me to get up, even though it meant emerging from my warm mummy bag.

Outside, we created a snowman, then ate breakfast: a hard-boiled egg, almonds, an apple, and a mug of tea made from melted snow.

As we departed, our footsteps screeched in the dry fresh snow and pine branches dusted us with powder as we brushed by. A mere few steps into the sunlight and onto grass and rocky terrain, our snowy wonderland was a memory. We headed north.

For me, not knowing where in the world I was, didn't matter. My steps were leading me on an adventure where one hill became another and eventually led to the crests and peaks that I saw in the view ahead. I was all in for the challenge. Most of the day we traversed *doglegs* above 9000 feet. *Doglegs* are the smaller hills that flow into and up to the main mountain like shoulders.

My boots were desirably stiff and provided good structure and support. This was a good thing because the technique for walking parallel to the incline required leaning uphill into the mountain, and digging-in slightly to grab the ground with the instep of my left foot and the outside of my right. This created a little shelf, the only weight bearing point to support myself plus the fifty-pound pack I humped.

Holt had the eye of a hunter. He noticed the slightest movement or most faint variation in color of the autumn palate. He'd freeze in his step, drop to a squat, and motion for me to follow. Then he'd scan the scenery with his binoculars. He spotted elk snacking in the bushes at a lower altitude. Around his neck, Holt wore a piece of ivory from his first elk kill dangling from a sinew cord. He'd thump his chest with his fist while clutching the tooth, then bow his head, and bring the tooth to his forehead--his way of honoring the dignified animal. We periodically spotted deer poised in the bush and taller grasses below us. Ptarmigan frequently skittered ahead of us as soon as they detected our approach. Matted animal paths crisscrossed the grassy slopes ahead.

We headed out early the next morning for the best chance of-stable weather. With only a few thousand feet to gain, the spine of the mountain was overhead. The peak was obscured by the rise in the terrain before and above us.

We left the tree line and crossed a grassy expanse. There, we laid our heavy packs aside a small snowmelt lake at about 11,800 feet. Then we set out to reach the peak with our lighter day packs. We carried only water, gorp (Good Ole Raisins and Nuts), and the gear necessary for potential weather and first aid.

We ascended the grassy slope, step over step due to its increasing steepness. Holt led the way, steadfast and surefooted. My pace lessened to the pull of gravity and the weight of my breath. He marched ahead and overhead on the bare slopes of gray solid rock. I looked up as Holt lifted out of sight several hundred feet in altitude above.

This was not a competition, except for within myself. Mid-chest my heartbeat thumped harder. I moved my focus to within. I had successfully persisted when things got tough in my life so I held certainty over the doubtful whispers that I would make the summit. Though, at this point, for me, each step—merely a toehold—required me to muster new momentum to initiate and complete it. I continued, little step, lift up, pause, little step, lift up, pause.

As I reached the horizontal undulating ground leading to the final ridge which stretched toward the summit, the hike became easier despite the altitude. My load seemed to lighten, my breath became more satisfying, and my hands reflexively raised up into the air as I loudly expressed my elation. "WoooHooo!"

The picture that Holt snapped from up ahead on the peak shows me back-dropped by the surrounding majesty of mountains. My bold red-gloved hands, with fingers splayed, reached into the sky with the little lake below. The exhilaration of my achievement after enduring and overcoming such an arduous feat made me feel like I earned my place amidst the grandeur.

I removed my day pack and left if for pick-up on the descent. The ridge to the final peak was a mound of rocky rubble. A cool wind gently pressed against me as I scrambled over the jags and crevasses.

Holt had an intimate reason for climbing to this location. He placed a dedication plaque to his former environmental activist soulmate who died from cancer. He completed the ceremony as I approached. We sat for a while in the absence of talking, at 13,054 feet. In this awe-filled, quiet realm, each was present with our own experience.

At this altitude, my mind was quiet and open as I experienced expansive wonder. Absent were the *shoulds* and *wouldas*. Gone was confusion and clutter. I felt released and relieved, like all was as it should be. There were no straight lines, no square edges—just interconnected patterns. There was nothing of the manmade, nothing of the logical, but rather all was natural, beautiful, with inherent intelligence and purpose. It was holistic. Mountains flowed into one another and up into the sky. Getting away *from it all* made the deeper relationship between all things more apparent. In awe, yet integrally immersed, I lost myself in the inclusiveness.

Since then, I have mused about my altitude adjustment and its positive altering effects on perception and attitude. There are common clichés which suggest bringing an elevated perspective to life and situations: *aim high*, *highlight for clarity*, *walk tall*, *take the high road*, and John Denver's insights to the *highs of the Rocky Mountains*. These all seem to be about getting outside of the box and transforming consciousness.

If altitude can help transcend limitation and open possibility, is it any wonder people seek to *get high*?

Barbara Young enjoys travel, almost always on the road less traveled. She hopes her stories in this years' NCPA Anthologies stir wanderlust, warm hearts, open opportunities and build bridges. In 2018 she published an empowerment book for nurses, *The Heart that Rocks Health Care,* and in 2019 was included in both volumes of NCPA's Anthologies, *Birds of a Feather* and *More Birds of a Feather.* In addition, Barbara also creates poetry, children's stories, plus gift and coffee table books that feature her photography.

Learn more at www.byoungbooks.com.

COME FLY WITH ME

CHRISTINE L. VILLA

For years, I had wanted to go to *Six Flags Discovery Kingdom* in Vallejo, California. No, it's not because I'm an adrenaline junkie who seeks heart-pumping thrill rides. It's because I'm a nature lover who likes to dream of flying with delicate, brightly-colored wings.

The moment I successfully uploaded the Six Flags app on my cell phone, the first thing I searched for was the *Butterfly Habitat*. It was disappointing to find out that it was located at the back of the amusement park. Thank God I wasn't with a child or an adult who couldn't wait to enjoy the rides that were categorized as kid-sized thrills, medium thrills, or maximum thrills. It was instead a leisurely walk with Lester, my ever-reliable traveling companion.

When we finally spotted the *Butterfly Shoppe*, a store for selling butterfly-themed souvenirs and gifts, I knew we had finally arrived. I trotted past the entrance and was instantly enthralled by butterflies flitting from one tropical plant to another. I thought I had to hunt for them with speed and agility. They were all around the place, darting from different directions, compelling me to immediately ignore a breathtaking koi pond and a waterfall.

I didn't mind walking through the glass atrium, which was humid and smelled like damp socks. I was lost in the moment, observing various butterfly species, such as swallowtails, birdwings, and brush-foots. Aside from being terrific acrobats, their vibrant colors were eye-catching and hypnotic. Before I knew it, I was chasing butterflies and taking pictures to my heart's content.

Lester soon left because of the humidity, but I was seemingly transported to another dimension. I was fixated on the blue butterflies, which would not perch on any leaf or branch close to me. For me, they stood out among the rest, not only because of their bigger size, but also because of their more elusive behavior. They fluttered by, inviting me to come fly with them.

Finally, I spotted a blue butterfly feeding on a rotten papaya that had been placed on a plate among the lush greenery. At first, I thought it wasn't one of the blue butterflies because as it sat feeding with its wings closed, the wings were brown. When they slightly opened for a few seconds, I caught a glimpse of the same blue color and pattern, which fascinated me at first.

So that was how it had been hiding from me for half an hour! I realized I had already taken a picture of it while it secretly perched on the bark of a tree with its camouflage ability.

Speaking of camouflage, a man wearing bright orange was walking around with a yellow-orange butterfly resting on his shoulder. I was one of the amused visitors taking pictures of this fortunate incident.

The man was laughing softly, perhaps hoping he could strut out of the atrium with his newfound friend. I knew that the big smile on his face would be short-lived because, by the exit door, someone would check each visitor to ensure that nobody had planned on bringing home a butterfly or had accidentally picked up a hitchhiker.

After realizing I had countless photos and a shirt soaked with sweat, I decided to join my travel buddy outside.

"Did you have enough?" Lester asked with a broad smile.

"Yes, but I disagree with the rating on their website. They posted the thrill level of the Butterfly Habitat as mild. No siree! It must be rated as heavenly!"

Christine L. Villa is a children's book author, poet, publisher, speaker, photographer, and mixed media artist. Among the eleven picture book titles she has published since 2014, seven have won awards in the Northern California Publishers and Authors Book Award Competitions, Royal Dragonfly Book Awards, Purple Dragonfly Book Awards, and Story Monsters Approved Book Awards. Her poems, photographs, and artwork have also won recognition and several awards. She is the founder of Purple Cotton Candy Arts, a business that offers publishing services to aspiring children's authors. She teaches a workshop entitled *Essentials of Writing a Picture Book*.

Chrissi is the founding editor of *Frameless Sky*, the first haiku and tanka journal available in DVD, and of Velvet Dusk Publishing.

You can learn more about Chrissi at www.christinevilla.com.

Other websites:
Publishing services for children's authors -
www.purplecottoncandyarts.com
Personal poetry website www.blossomrain.blogspot.com
Poetry journal accepting submissions -
www.framelesssky.weebly.com
Publishing services for poets -
www.velvetduskpublishing.com

THE EXTRAORDINARY MT. RUSHMORE ENCOUNTER

CHARLENE JOHNSON

"**D**on't go too far, kids," Felicity called after the twins. "We won't, Mama," the twins, Abigail and Alexander, answered in unison.

Dex leaned back on the blanket, watching them disappear through a thicket of trees, their laughter echoing through the forest. "I'm glad we decided to make this trip to Mt. Rushmore."

"Me too."

"I can't believe the twins are already six years old. Seems like it was just yesterday we were rushing you to the hospital."

Felicity nodded, picking up a grape and popping it into her mouth. "That was quite the adventure."

"I'm glad your parents' flight was delayed and they missed the uproar."

She laughed. "Who would have thought our kids would shift so soon after birth and disappear from the hospital nursery? I'm sorry I missed the whole thing but the medication they gave me knocked me out. Being a protective new mother, I would have panicked."

"I don't think I ever told you the entire story."

Felicity settled against his shoulder. "You did, but you can tell me again. I never tire of hearing the story of our twins' first day."

"The head nurse on duty came to me in a panic telling me our twins were missing. She ordered the other nurses on the nursery floor station and the security guards to comb the entire hospital to find them."

"Your parents were there. What did they do?"

"They helped me look for them. We were sure we knew what happened."

"How long did it take you to find them?"

Dex chuckled. "Not long. There was only one place in the hospital I thought they might go. I had no idea what creatures they had shifted into. That scared me a little. What if the security guards shot first and asked questions later?

"My parents and I got to the courtyard garden before the security guards did. There was an automatic door at the entrance. That's how the twins entered. You should have seen the priceless looks of astonishment on the security guards' faces when they saw two baby foxes running around the Chinese maple trees."

"Thank goodness you were there to intervene."

"The twins saw me and jumped into my arms, licking my face. Stunned the guards completely."

Felicity laughed. "I would have loved to have seen that. What explanation did you give for being so chummy with two wild animals?"

"I told the security guards I was a nature enthusiast and had an uncanny affinity with animals. I volunteered to take the little foxes to a local animal rescue shelter. Luckily, there was one close by."

"How did you get the twins to shift back?"

Dex smiled. "I took them to our SUV and told them if they didn't shift back, their mama would be very upset."

Felicity gazed up at him. "They listened?"

"Believe it or not, they understood and shifted. I bought them back in the hospital."

"That's when you brought them to my room," she added.

"Yes. You were asleep and the twins didn't make a sound. Then I went to alert the head nurse on duty, and she called the search off. They never figured out how the twins got in your room, but they tightened up their hospital security measures after that."

"That's what we get for going to a hospital for humans."

Dex shrugged. "We didn't have a choice. Your contractions were too close to get to your regular doctor's office."

"I love that story. We'll have to tell the kids when they are older," Felicity said, suddenly sitting up and looking around. "Speaking of the twins. I don't hear them."

"They're probably playing hide and seek." Dex stood up. "I'll go look for them."

*   *   *

For the twins' sixth birthday, Dex and Felicity decided to take them on a camping trip. It would give them the opportunity to shift and run freely. They'd thought about taking them to Disneyland since Abigail and Alexander were just starting to be able to control their shifts, but it still wasn't foolproof. All they needed was for the twins to shift on the Jungle Cruise or the Pirates of the Caribbean rides. What a disaster that would have been.

Dex's parents suggested this campsite. They had used it multiple times over the years. Too primitive and secluded, not many tourists were willing to camp there since it had no amenities. It was just the kind of place Dex and Felicity preferred. It gave them the freedom to shift without being seen. There was a creek within walking distance and a vast forest for their family to roam yards away.

It was well worth the drive. It took fifteen hours to drive from their farm outside of Colville to the campsite not far from Mt. Rushmore National Park. They pitched a two-room tent before dark and had been at the campsite for two days. In that time, the only person they saw was a fish and game officer on an ATV. They were truly alone.

"I can't find the kids," Dex said as he jogged back to the campfire.

Felicity immediately became alarmed, her motherly instinct kicking in.

Dex saw the expression on her face. "Don't worry. They may have shifted and gone too far and lost their way back. Their senses aren't as developed as ours. I'm sure they're looking for the camp as we speak."

"I hope you're right. Abigail and Alexander are too

215

young to be out in the forest alone."

It was starting to get dark and the fog was slowly drifting in. Soon, they wouldn't be able to see beyond their campfire. They'd have to rely on their senses.

"I can shift to a bald eagle or an owl," Felicity suggested. "I may be able to see them through the trees."

"It's nearly dark and the forest is too dense, honey. Finding them while in the sky will be impossible. We would have a better chance in wolf form. Their senses are more acute at night, giving us an advantage."

The wolves followed the scent of the twins away from the camp through the forest for miles to the outskirts of Mt. Rushmore National Park. It was October and the park closed at 9:00 p.m. Fortunately, it was almost 8:30 p.m. and there were no tourists about.

How had the twins strayed so far? Dex thought, his wolf ear's pricking up in alarm. The twins preferred to shift to wolf pups. He sniffed the air and picked up their scent for the first time in an hour. It was getting stronger. They had to be close.

Felicity padded up beside him, emitting a low whine. Dex nuzzled her neck, trying to comfort her. She leaned into him, rubbing her snout against his.

A sudden otherworldly howl made the hair on the back of Dex's neck bristle. It was an eerie sound he'd never heard before. He was on immediate alert. What animal was it?

Dex padded toward the sound with Felicity following closely behind. There was movement in a thicket of trees below the monument. Peeking out from behind a tall redwood tree below the carved image of George Washington was a large, hairy figure. It stood upright as it peered out then dashed behind another tree. Had he just seen Bigfoot?

Before the trip, Dex had found an article online about tourists seeing an enormous hairy creature staring at them from the cover of large redwood trees near the park, but each time it disappeared into the dense thicket before the tourists could snap a photo. At the time, he discounted the stories. He and his brothers had roamed through the forest all his life and never encountered one. Neither had his parents.

The whimper of wolf pups interrupted his thoughts. The sounds were coming from the direction of the creature. Growling low and sniffing the air, Dex picked up a foreign scent. It had to be the creature.

Dex crept along the path and up the incline, keeping close to the ground as he tried to quickly assess the creature's potential threat to the twins. He bared his canines as his growl grew louder. The thought of them being in any danger incensed him.

Bounding around the trees and over rocks, he was nearing the last place he saw the creature. Felicity was trailing behind as his strides widened. Stopping when he reached the tree, he realized there was no scent present and no creature. The creature had vanished.

He could no longer smell the twins' scent or hear their whines. The twins were gone.

*   *   *

With no additional scent of the creature or the wolf pups to follow, Dex and Felicity hurried back to their camp. They shifted back and quickly got dressed, planning to drive closer to the park to continue their search. But worried the twins may show up at their campsite, Felicity chose to stay behind. Dex went alone.

He parked the car in a hotel parking lot in Keystone and would hike in the rest of the way. He retrieved his duffle bag out of the SUV and locked the door.

When he got near the park gates, he looked around for a safe place to shift.

"Hello, friend," a man with long jet-black hair, dressed in blue jeans and a black tee greeted.

Dex spun around and regarded the man with suspicion. Where had he come from? He didn't hear him approach. The man was clearly American Indian and someone of note given the elaborate medicine bag that hung around his neck. Possibly a medicine man.

"Who are you?" Dex asked.

"My name is Eddie **Howahkan, I'm a** Shaman, a healer to my people, the Lakotas."

Dex glanced at the grove of trees where he had planned to shift. He didn't have time for a casual conversation. He had to find the twins.

He flung his duffle over his shoulder. "I'm sorry. I'm in a hurry so if you don't mind…"

"I saw you earlier in the shape of a wolf. You were pursuing the great giant of our forest. We call him *Chiye-tanka. The white man calls him Bigfoot."*

Dex didn't know what to say. How did this man know what he was and why was he there?

"I mean you no harm. I know what you are. You and your mate are more than sunkmanitu tanka, the sacred wolf. You are shapeshifters. I've known many over the years."

"Were you watching us?"

"Not intentionally. I come here to pay homage to our forgotten dead."

The shaman's words rang true. Dex felt no threat. He held out his hand. "I apologize. I rarely meet anyone who knows what I am. I'm Dex Brooks."

"What were you looking for?"

"Our children. Twins. Six years old. They went off to play in the forest where we are camped and never returned. We assumed they shifted, and were able to track them to the vicinity of the monument. That's where I saw Bigfoot. Until that moment, I didn't believe they existed."

"The Lakota have known of their existence for many centuries. They are our brothers."

"Do you think one of them would take our twins? They were in wolf form."

Eddie shook his head. "No. They only kill to feed their families, much like we do. Deer, elk, and occasionally bison that stray from the Badlands. If one of the *Chiye-tanka* has them it is because he is trying to protect them."

"There are more than one?"

"Yes," Eddie replied. "There are many."

"Do you know where I can find them?" Dex asked. "I

must find out if our kids are with them."

"Yes, I can take you to their hidden compound."

"I'd like to drive to our campsite and get my wife before we go."

Eddie nodded. "I'll follow you there. It would be an honor to meet her."

A half hour later, Dex and Felicity followed Eddie in their SUV, hopeful to find their twins.

They drove well into the mountains up a steep, dirt road that would have been unpassable after a serious rain. Eddie made a right off the dirt road, between a dense coppice of redwood trees.

"We'll have to go on foot from here," Eddie advised. "This is not a place even the most seasoned hikers come to, especially in the dark. Too many reports of apex predators who hunt in this area."

The trio hiked for two miles past boulders and trees along the cliff face until they reached an area where two large boulders formed a hidden entry. Eddie walked between the boulders and through a structure of interlacing tree limbs that formed a long leafy canopy.

Crude wooden cabins formed a circle around an enormous rock-lined campfire. Females were busy preparing wooden bowls of fruits and vegetables and placing them on a long log table while children played throughout the trees and into the courtyard. Large males with freshly butchered meat hoisted on their shoulders laid their bounty on log tables while other males skewered the meat on long sharp wooden poles and placed them over the open fire. It was clear they had a thriving community – one that was so unique humans have tried to document their existence for decades.

"I bring them supplies when I come to the park," Eddie said as he sat down the large backpack. "Things they can't harvest in the woods. In return, they give me smoked venison and elk to take back to the reservation."

"They are not much different from us," Felicity observed.

Eddie smiled. "No, they're not."

*　*　*

A massive male emerged from the largest cabin near the center of the village. He must have been eight feet tall. He towered over many of the males working busily by the fire. Seeing Eddie, Dex, and Felicity, he strode in their direction, his powerful arms swinging with each step.

"That's Samuel," Eddie whispered. "He's their leader. I've known him for more than thirty years. Let me introduce you to him."

Samuel stared at Dex and Felicity with curious eyes. "You know we don't like visitors here, Eddie. Especially human ones."

Eddie held out his hand and Samuel shook it. "I know but this is a very special circumstance."

Samuel frowned. "What do you mean?"

"Dex and Felicity are more than humans. They are shapeshifters, much like Skinwalkers. They're looking for their children."

Samuel nodded. "But why come here? My people don't steal children. We are a peaceful species who want to live away from the prying eyes of nosy humans. With TV shows like *Expedition Bigfoot* and that movie, *Harry and the Hendersons,* human researchers are everywhere looking for our kind. We've had to be extremely cautious when foraging for food of late."

"Our children were playing near our campsite and wandered off," Dex responded. "Felicity and I tracked them to the trees below the monument. We believe they shifted into wolf cubs. I heard their whines and saw one of your people peeking out from behind a tree. When we reached that area, no one was there."

Samuel chuckled. "They must be the wolf cubs Steven brought back with him. He assumed they got separated from their mother. He was planning to find their pack in the morning. We fed them and they're sleeping in my cabin."

"Our babies are safe!" Felicity exclaimed, hugging her husband.

"Thank you, Samuel!" Dex said over his wife's head.

Felicity turned to him and smiled. "Thank you!"

"Steven," Samuel shouted.

One of the males near the fire padded up to them. "You have need of me?"

"These are the wolf cubs' parents."

Steven's eyebrows shot up in surprise. "But..."

Samuel laughed, putting up a hand. "I'll explain later. Could you get them? Their parents are anxious to see them."

"Yes, Samuel."

"May I ask a question?" Felicity asked.

"Of course," Samuel answered.

"How did you learn to speak?"

"We adapted eons ago." Samuel inclined his head to Eddie. "The Indians have always been respectful to us. We've co-existed peacefully since the beginning of our creation. We've learned much from them, including the ability to speak. Humans believe we can't speak. It's not that we can't but we just prefer not to."

When the wolf cubs emerged from Samuel's cabin and saw Dex and Felicity, they struggled to get out of Steven's massive arms. He leaned down and let them go. They scampered to their parents, jumping up and down. One moment they were wolf cubs, the next moment they were children again, hugging their parents.

Dex pulled out his backpack and Felicity helped the kids dress.

"We're sorry," Alexander apologized. "Me and Abbie went too far and we couldn't find our way back. It was getting dark, and we got really scared."

Abigail pointed to Steven. "He found us and brought us to his home. He said he would help us find you."

Felicity hugged them. "You must be more careful. You don't know this forest as you do ours at home."

"We know, Mama," the twins said in unison.

"As you get older, your senses will become more acute," Dex added. "You will always be able to find your way to us."

"Thank you, Steven," Felicity said gratefully, "for keeping them safe."

Steven smiled. "No problem. I'm glad I could help."

Dex took Alexander's hand. "We should be going, Samuel. We've imposed on you enough."

"Why not stay and eat with us?" Samuel offered. "I haven't seen Eddie in a while, and you can tell us all about your family of shapeshifters. Staying so isolated, we've never met one of your kind. I've had a few encounters with Skinwalkers who have passed through our territory. A nasty lot. Not anything you ever want to come face to face with."

"Skinwalkers are associated with the Navajo and are found in the southwest. They rarely travel this far north." Eddie added. "We do have our own legends such as the Iktomi."

"Iktomi?" Dex asked.

"The word Iktomi means spider and is sometimes called spiderman. He's often depicted as a man who behaves most inappropriately by our Lakota standards. Many stories about the Iktomi are funny,) but there are some that speak of serious or violent behavior."

"Skinwalkers and the Iktomi sound like creatures to steer clear of," Dex interjected. "As for your gracious invitation, Samuel, we accept."

After meeting the other members of Samuel's extended family and sharing a delicious dinner, Dex, Felicity and the twins said their goodbyes.

"If you are ever back in this part of the country, please be sure to have Eddie bring you here to see us," Samuel said.

Dex shook his hand. "We will. Samuel. Again, thank you for everything."

Dex and his family followed Eddie back to their campsite. The twins were sound asleep. After getting them settled in their sleeping bags, Felicity offered Eddie a cup of coffee before he headed back home.

"Eddie, we are so glad we met you. If not for you, we may have never found the twins."

Eddie waved their words away. "I merely led you to the

one who found them."

"Be assured, we will protect Samuel's secret," Dex pledged. "We worry every time we're in the forest that someone will see us shift and expose us to the world. We totally understand his need for secrecy."

"I never doubted you'd keep their secret. We Lakota have many secrets of our own."

Eddie stood up and handed the coffee cup to Felicity. "I'd better head out. I have a long drive back to the reservation."

"Thank you again, Eddie," Dex said. "Have a safe journey home."

"Goodbye, Eddie," Felicity added, shaking his hand.

Eddie grinned. "We Lakotas never say goodbye. We say Doksa ake waunkte – I will see you again."

"Doksa ake waunkte," Dex and Felicity repeated.

As they watched Eddie's truck drive away, the disappearance of the twins and the shocking discovery of Bigfoot's existence were front and center on their minds. They had the most extraordinary encounter on their trip to Mt. Rushmore, one they would never forget.

"I thought Grandma Hannah's admission she was a shapeshifter at Thanksgiving was the shock of the century."

Dex put his arm around Felicity and laughed. "I think meeting a Bigfoot, tops that – at least for now."

"Maybe we'll find the Loch Ness monster exists too," Felicity teased.

Dex grinned. "We'll leave that adventure for our next vacation."

Charlene Johnson lives on a farm outside of Colville, Washington.

Her Published Works:

Paranormal Romance
Circle of the Red Scorpion series - *Shattered, Avenged, Dawned, Returned, Awakened*
Circle of the Red Scorpion World series - *Damned*

Romantic Suspense
Sterling Wood series – *Homecoming, Changing the Rules*
Crimes of Passion series - *Blown Away*

Charlene also published nine short stories for various anthologies.

She has received the following awards:
Four Book Excellence Finalist awards
Two Literary Titan Silver Awards
One Literary Titan Gold Award
One Readers Favorite Five Star Award

Besides reading and writing, she also enjoys photography, travel, music, bird watching and Elvis.

Her quote - *I've traveled the world, crossed galaxies, traveled through time and explored history on the pages of books.*

Websites:
https://www.charlenejohnsonbooks.com
https://www.circleoftheredscorpion.com
https://www.sterlingwoodseries.com

Email:
circleoftheredscorpion@gmail.com

NCPA * OUR PURPOSE * WHO WE ARE * WHAT WE DO

Northern California Publishers & Authors (NCPA) is an alliance of independent publishers, authors, and publishing professionals in Northern California.

Formed in 1991 as Sacramento Publishers Association, then expanded to Sacramento Publishers and Authors and eventually to NCPA, our purpose is to foster, encourage, and educate authors, small publishers, and those interested in becoming authors and publishers.

Service providers who cater to the publishing industry – illustrators, cover designers, editors, etc. – are also invited to join NCPA as associate members.

We support small indie presses, self-publishers and aspiring authors at our monthly meetings by covering topics such as self- and traditional publishing, editing, book design, author-related tax and legal issues, and marketing.

In addition to our annual NCPA Book Anthology, for _members only_, which started again in 2019, NCPA holds an annual Book Awards Competition for both _members, and non-members._ The NCPA Book Awards Competition celebrated our 28th year in June, with the entry of 27 books published in 2021.

NCPA has also given back to the community through proceeds from a Silent Auction during our Book Awards Banquets in the form of $1000 to: a scholarship to a college-bound, local high school senior intending to pursue a publishing or writing-related degree; 916-Ink, which empowers youth through the published, written word; Mustard Seed School for underprivileged youth; and Friends of the Sacramento Public Library, which provides books to the homes of underprivileged children. Proceeds for the upcoming year will again go to Friends of the Sacramento Public Library.

Check out our website www.norcalpa.org for current information on our meetings, how to join NCPA, about our next Book Awards Competition, and upcoming anthologies.

OTHER NCPA ANTHOLOGIES

Purchase anthologies at Amazon, Samati Press, or in person from any author in the BEAUTIFUL AMERICAS anthology. Anthologies are also available in eBook format. Information on each author in all anthologies can be found on the NCPA website: www.norcalpa.org

BIRDS OF A FEATHER
An NCPA Anthology

A Collection of Short Stories about Animals

From their size, color, and the way they see the world, animals are diverse—and so are the delightful stories in this anthology. Ranging from legends and true tales of wildland bears to a memorable veterinary house call and stories of humans who become animals (or act like them), this collection is all about animals and our relationships with them. Meet rabbits, lizards, guinea pigs, potbelly pigs, horses, seals, owls, spiders, coyotes, wolves, elephants, and of course plenty of cats and dogs who will touch your heart and remind you that no matter how many legs we have, we all have much in common.

MORE BIRDS OF A FEATHER
An NCPA ANTHOLOGY
A Collection of Short Stories about Animals and Other Things

Within these pages are thirty non-fiction stories—some happy, some sad; some exciting, some glad; some daring, some caring— about a variety of animals. Add a little fiction: one far-out adventure and one fantasy, then toss in a couple of on-going series, previously introduced in *Birds of a Feather*.

There's Nacht, our resident feral cat who presents Tux, then our fun shape-shifters Dex and Felicity as the red fox and Arctic fox. Meet two elk and three penguins; a bunny that wouldn't give up; two elephants; a goat on the run; a potty-trained pig; two squirrels; and a bunch of wild birds, including a gosling, plus tame chickens: Lady Cluck and her girls; lizards in the Caribbean; crickets; a gorilla; a bear; a tortoise; and a variety of cats and dogs.

And a partridge in a pear tree? Maybe not, but the second NCPA anthology from 2019 is a lot of chirping fun.

DESTINATION: THE WORLD

Volume One

NCPA Anthology 2020

a collection of short stories about travel/vacations

Take a journey around the world with 35 authors from NCPA as they share their stories covering nearly every continent and a vast array of cultures. This collection of charming and endearing tales will take you on excursions beyond your own backyard from breathtaking trips of a lifetime to harrowing adventures and comical misadventures.

Enjoy more than thirty non-fiction stories, including: A Long-awaited Trip to Greece * "Wogging" in Ireland * China by Train * Ghosts in BC * and a First-Time Flight from Nigeria to America. If you're looking for fiction, discover the secret behind *Lance's Toboggan of Miracles,* follow the further adventures of Nacht, the Wanderer who stops wandering, and continue the fantasy adventures of our favorite shape-shifters, Dex and Felicity (introduced in NCPA's 2019 anthologies: *Birds of a Feather* and *More Birds of a Feather*), as they take their romance on the road with a honeymoon in Hawaii.

DESTINATION: THE WORLD
Volume Two

NCPA Anthology 2020
a collection of short
stories about
travel/vacations

Following an epic year marred by a pandemic, NCPA introduces *Destination: The World, Volume Two*, an anthology filled with travel accounts and fun experiences.

Enjoy more than thirty stories, including: the Loma Prieta earthquake; a missing earring in Williamsburg, VA; a trip to Havana, Cuba; a mistaken identity in Italy; a little girl learns a lesson in humanities. Find how a sanctuary in Scotland led to the battlefield in NY in 1758. Join a "sneaky boy" when he becomes a stowaway child aboard a ship migrating from Spain in 1907; thrill to a search for weapons in Israel; a close-call on the Zambezi, and a near arrest in Italy.

Featuring the 4th installment in two of our series: the red Fox and the Arctic Fox, our favorite shape-shifters, Dex and Felicity, as they meet the Menehunes, and loveable Nacht, the feral cat. Let your heart be warmed when Nacht meets his forever human.

Destination: The World, Volume Two, covers it all from A to Z: America to Zimbabwe, and everywhere in-between. Immerse yourself in this diverse, one-of-a-kind NCPA Anthology.

All
Holidays
2020

AN NCPA ANTHOLOGY
FIRST ANNUAL

Our cover indicates winter holidays, but NCPA offers this warning: "Don't Judge a Book by its Cover". ALL Holidays means exactly that, ALL HOLIDAYS. NCPA's 1st Annual *ALL Holidays 2020* anthology includes a variety of traditional and non-traditional holidays from New Year's Day to New Year's Eve, with celebrations from many lands, religions, and cultures.

Our beloved cat Nacht returns telling stories to a new batch of ferals, and Dex and Felicity, our favorite shape-shifting foxes are back with a new adventure. For the first time we also introduce poetry in all forms: from rhyming and free form, to traditional and non-traditional Haiku, plus Haikai, Haibun, Renga and Cherita.

NCPA's First Holiday Anthology is packed as full as a Christmas stocking with enjoyable stories and entertaining traditions. Look for a second annual *ALL Holidays 2021* coming soon!

Our 2ⁿᵈ ALL Holidays volume returns with stories, flash fiction and more poems: free-form, rhyming, Haiku, and split sequence. Visit traditional and non-traditional celebrations from 30 authors sharing holidays from Thanksgiving to Purple Heart Day.

Back for the 6ᵗʰ time, series favorites, semi-feral Nacht complains about fireworks. Dex and Felicity, our romantic shapeshifter foxes with two happy surprises. More romance in the air thanks to a power outage in Washington.

A young boy's wish comes true. Another's belief in Santa is prolonged. Caribbean funky amphibian shoes. Good Shepherd pendant. A meaningful box of stamped, blank cards. A play at a small school in the 60s. A visit from Humpty. One final celebration with Beethoven.

NCPA's Second Holiday anthology is as stuffed with fun and entertaining stories as the turkey is with dressing.

Made in the USA
Middletown, DE
30 November 2022